MY
AWE-INSPIRING
JOURNEY

MY
AWE-INSPIRING
JOURNEY

Teresita Lipsius

Order this book online at www.trafford.com
or email orders@trafford.com

Most Trafford titles are also available at major online book retailers.

Printed in the United States of America.

ISBN: 978-1-4669-0667-9 (sc)
ISBN: 978-1-4669-0666-2 (hc)
ISBN: 978-1-4669-0668-6 (e)

Library of Congress Control Number: 2011963218

Trafford rev. 12/23/2011

 www.trafford.com

North America & international
toll-free: 1 888 232 4444 (USA & Canada)
phone: 250 383 6864 ♦ fax: 812 355 4082

CHAPTER 1

I would like to share with you my amazing journey through life so far.

My father was a military man who fought against the Japanese during World War II. He belonged to a battalion that had gone to the province of Leyte in the Visayan region of the Philippines. As a result, he was a very rigid and disciplined man who ran his family as if we were a military unit. We always had to be prompt or else face the consequences. He hated people being late, especially for appointments or meals. He felt that it was an insult to the host if one was late to a dinner or party.

Papa would often reminisce about the war when I and my sister were young, telling us about what had happened to him—the hardships on the battlefield, not knowing whether he would come back to the garrison and be with his comrades again. He would say, "In the battlefield, nobody would think of anything except to fight for his country and fight for his life. It was survival of the fittest." However, the tales of his war experiences diminished with time, and after we started high school, Papa hardly mentioned them any more.

My mother had enlisted in the Women's Auxiliary and been assigned to the same garrison as Papa. There were heavy casualties, and all women's auxiliaries were utilized. Papa brought some badly injured soldiers, one of whom was my mother's brother, to the garrison, and that was how my parents met. Their love blossomed, and in 1944, right after the war, they were married. My sister Alma was born first, and then two years later I came out into the world.

I was born in Aloguinsan, a municipality in the province of Cebu in the Philippines. My Papa was a policeman who would proudly report to work wearing his highly starched khaki uniform and carrying a *porras* (baton) in his hand. Mama was working toward her Bachelor of Education degree at the University of the Visayas (UV), one of the oldest universities in the Cebu province, which was a two-hour drive from Aloguinsan.

The town had been created by virtue of a royal decree by the king of Spain in 1886. The first captain was my mother's great-uncle, Felomino Nengasca. He became "Captain Municipal". The town was named according to the following tale. In the early days of the Spanish colonial period, a soldier of the Spanish Royal Audiencia (court) happened to be in the vicinity of what is now the town centre. Being a stranger to the place, the soldier wanted to know the name of the area and asked a passing fisherman in Spanish, "*Como se llama este lugar?*" The Filipino fisherman thought the soldier had asked about the name of the fish catch he was carrying, and he answered, "*Kinsan*". The soldier, not hearing properly, repeated his question, and the fisherman, who was carrying just a large fish head, elaborated, "Ulo sa kinsan", which has changed into its present name, *Aloguinsan*.

Aloguinsan in the fifties and sixties was very isolated, with only two buses travelling between it and Cebu, the closest city. If you missed the last bus, you had to wait until the next day to get home. I love my town, so peaceful and green. Back then you could hear guys and gals, old and young, laughing and telling old jokes in the middle of the street. Mama would say to Papa, "Ling (Papa's pet name), go and play your harp." As soon as our friends and neighbours heard Papa's music, they would come dancing from all directions, laughing as though drunk, while Mama sang beautifully, accompanied by my father's expert fingers strumming his harp. Mama was a church choir coordinator and member until her late eighties.

There was no electricity, only street lamps fuelled by kerosene. No radio or any sort of communication or entertainment, like the cinema or television, existed. There was an occasional "mobile theatre", which would make us all *extremely* excited when we heard the mobile van announcing, "There will be a movie showing in the town plaza tonight." The van would go all round the town to all suburbs, announcing the movie event through a loudspeaker. As Nang Bating, one of the old folk in town would say: "Hush, people! Listen to the speaker-loud!"

The man on the loudspeaker would announce, "Folks, have dinner early. The movie starts at six thirty in the evening. Be prompt!" He would be accompanied by deafening background music, which inspired everyone, despite the fact that it was so loud that even the deafest deaf and the century-old corpses in the cemetery could hear it. This was more than enough to put Aloguinsan into party mode. You cannot imagine the excitement of the children like me—and not only the children, but adults as well—when they watched an American cowboy movie which had probably been filmed at least several decades before. For the people of Aloguinsan, it was a real treat!

There were no telephones in Aloguinsan until the eighties. Our only communication with the outside world was by telegraph (Morse code). This was an amazingly accurate form of communication, usually allowing us to be up to date with the news around the Philippines. We were more behind the times with the world at large, but we definitely knew what was going on in our own country.

It was the practice in the Philippines at that time to starch all clothes, even the underwear—and especially any uniforms. I distinctly remember Nang Benig, the laundry lady, boiling a big pot of water, pouring what seemed to me like kilograms of starch powder into it, stirring until it looked like a Chinese bird's nest soup, and then pouring it into a huge basin. She would then soak Papa's khaki uniforms, and any of our other clothes which needed washing, in this mix for a few minutes. She made sure each piece of clothing was evenly starched. When she was satisfied, she would squeeze out the clothing before hanging it out to dry. As there was no electricity, people used charcoal to heat a flat iron to press the clothes. It was a hollow *v*-shaped iron with a wooden handle; the hot charcoal would be placed in the hollow. Nang Benig used it to iron all our clothes, including Papa's police uniforms. The result—use your imagination! Imagine underwear as stiff as the cloths wrapped around an Egyptian mummy. However, people wore them without any sign of discomfort.

There was no official bakery in town. People made their own bread, biscuits, and *salvaros*, flat bread made of shredded coconut, flour, yeast, and brown sugar. All were baked in a clay oven, which was moulded like a big basin and covered with a removable sheet of galvanized iron. However, Tiya Ponting, from next door, was our town's favourite baker, supplying home-baked bread and *puto sulot* (a fried bread coated with caramel) around the town. She would build a fire with old, dry wood at the bottom of the clay oven, collect some of the embers, and put them on top of the galvanized iron cover. There was an opening in the front, which was closed during baking time. Two huge wooden spatulas were used for turning and removing the bread from the oven. Then Tiya's sister, Inday Delay, would take it and go around the streets singing out: *"Sulot in it pa"* (hot sulot).

People in Aloguinsan knew everyone in town and were traditionally helpful and friendly—except at election time, which occurred every three years. Local elections were everyone's nightmare. People were diehards with their candidates and would do anything to help them win an election. I'm sad to say that it split families and friends apart, with feuds lasting for years.

There are two major events in the Aloguinsan calendar: the town fiesta and Holy Week. These celebrations go to the extreme. The town fiesta is a week-long carnival, beginning on 15 October and finishing on the twenty-fourth. It is our tradition that on the eve of the fiesta, at about six o'clock, devotees march all over town, followed by a lavishly decorated carriage carrying Archangel San Raphael. This, in turn, is followed by a military band, hired by the council to assist with the mass, the *retreta* (or dawn march) along the streets, and for the night's activities. During this carnival there are beauty pageants, floats, and most importantly, a procession. On the final day, Aloguinsan celebrates the town's patron saint, San Raphael. Everyone is as jolly as they can be. After each fiesta, people start raising piglets to grow them to the right size for the spit roast dedicated to our patron saint. Fiesta for the locals will never be complete unless they have a traditional *inasal* (spit roast), a Filipino delicacy, to serve to their guests.

Holy Week is different. Nearly everyone is sober. It begins on Palm Sunday and ends on Easter Sunday. People in Aloguinsan and nationwide observe Holy Week wholeheartedly, especially Good Friday, when everything is closed. That is our way of saying sorry for our sins, and it is when we pray for all the people in the world, our families, and ourselves. We thank God for everything He has given us. At midday, people gather in front of the church. Then they listen to the *siete palabras* (seven last words), which finishes at exactly three o'clock in the afternoon, the time that Christ died on the cross.

All radio stations (most households had radios in the late seventies) were shut off until after the *sugat* (meeting of Christ and His mother) on Easter Sunday. I am not a fanatic, but I believe strongly that God loves, protects, helps, and guides me wherever I go and whatever I do. I was born and baptized in a Roman Catholic Church in Aloguinsan, Cebu, Philippines, as Teresita Garing Pielago, and I will remain faithful to my religion here on earth until the end of my life.

The Philippines has one of the highest literacy rates in Asia. About 85 to 90 per cent of people can read and write, and about 98 per cent of school-aged children attend school, with 30 per cent continuing on to college. Most Filipino families regard education as a means of improving their lives; it is an asset to the parents. The educational experience for many students starts with six years of primary education provided free in public schools. This is followed by four years of secondary school and, for some, four to five years of college education.

The first moment I vividly remember was in 1954, when I started as a Grade 1 student in our local primary school. For four years, Nang Alma and I boarded with our grandparents, who also looked after our cousins, Wellie, Serena, and Dulcie, who had lost their mothers to cancer in the same year.

Miss Echavez, my Grade 1 teacher, taught a class of fifty pupils, as there was no kindergarten at that time. I remember her as being a bit round, grumpy, but not bad looking. For some reason, she never married and remained a spinster until she died. She had a habit of carrying a stick for dual purposes: pointing to letters of the alphabet on the board, and hitting our hands if we misbehaved and would not write the alphabet properly. It was routine to have one or two action songs before class each morning and to finish off in the afternoon with another song. The song in the afternoon was "Goodbye, my teacher, goodbye. We will come back again. Goodbye, my teacher, goodbye." When Miss Echavez had been grumpy, we would alter this to "We will *not* come back again."

I was not a bright student, just average, and a little bit shy. However, Miss Echavez would say, "Teresita, it is your turn to lead the action song, 'I Have

Two Hands'." She knew it was my favourite song and that I had learned it by heart.

> *I hab to hands, the let and the right.*
> *Hol de na pie so kle a bry,*
> *Clap dem sotly one to tre,*
> *Clean litol hands are good to see.*

It was one of my proudest moments, and I felt as if I had won a golden Oscar. I carried that triumph for years. Mama was also thrilled, and she asked me to sing it often—at full volume, of course—and with the actions. She would ask me to repeat the second line. "Hold them up high, so clean and bright," Mama would say. It took a few months for me to properly pronounce the words of this song.

My high school years at the Santa Ana Academy were an unforgettable experience. This was in the neighbouring town of Barili, in the north-west of Cebu province, a one hour drive from Aloguinsan. I was very happy, content, and comfortable with my new surroundings and my newfound friends—especially my everlasting friend Silay. Silay's aunt, Miss Lena, was a very dear friend and colleague of my mother's. She suggested that my sister and I enrol in the Santa Ana Academy and offered to have us stay in her family's home. My parents happily agreed.

Nang Saria, Miss Lena's mother, was incredible, full of love and very protective. She accepted me and treated me like her own granddaughter. Silay, her real granddaughter, was a godsend. She was few years younger than I was, but we clicked as if we were identical twins. We travelled together, we cried and laughed together. We are still very close, despite the physical distance separating us today.

In my sophomore year at the Academy, one of the core subjects was biology. Our teacher, Miss Carampatana, was brilliant and one of the best science teachers in the province of Cebu. Although biology was my favourite subject, it became a nightmare, as my little brain just could not memorize an entire phylum. My frustration was echoed and shared by two of my closest friends and classmates, Tessie and Micmic. In our frustration, we made up a phylum, *Phylum Carampatana*, using our teacher's name!

In the middle of the third term, all third-year biology students were scheduled to dissect a frog as their final practical exam. We had to review the whole chapter about frog's hearts, including the right and left ventricle. There were four in my group: Tessie, Micmic, Cressie, and myself as the leader. To get a frog was another nightmare. We had to get our own, as they were not supplied by the school, so the children living in the area surrounding our school would find frogs and sell them to biology students for a very high price.

The day arrived for our exam. Although we had had demonstrations, closely supervised by Miss Carampatana, the four of us were very unsure about whether we could do this. Each of us had a job to perform; Micmic and I were to dissect the heart of the frog and locate the large ventricle. As the leader, I was supposed to be brave and knowledgeable; however, my hands would not stop shaking, and I found the sight of the blood very disturbing. Then, to my surprise, we found what we needed to find—the large ventricle! However, because it had taken so long for us to investigate the parts of the heart, the frog died. We suspected the poor thing had had a heart attack. I felt as if all eyes were on me, angrily blaming me for killing the frog, which I certainly hadn't intended to do. Luckily, we were able to reschedule the exam for the following week, and we successfully completed the dissection the second time round.

Our graduation day was in April 1968. It was hard to believe four enchanting years had passed. Saying goodbye to teachers, classmates, and especially to the other two in our awesome threesome—Micmic and Tessie—was difficult to endure. Our friendship had grown stronger and stronger over the four years of high school. Sadly, the three of us went our separate ways after graduation. We enrolled in different universities, we met new friends, and gradually our bond dwindled.

A fresh graduate from high school would usually enrol straightaway at a university in the city. I enrolled at the University of San Carlos (USC), one of the oldest universities in the Philippines, which is run by Divine Word Missionaries (SVD) fathers. I took preparatory subjects for one year, as I was not certain what particular field I wanted to continue in.

While I was at university, I lived in a boarding house in Cebu City, in V. Rama Street, not far from my friend Silay's grandfather. Cebu City is the commercial and educational centre of the Visayas and is the oldest city in the Philippines, having been founded by Spaniards in 1565. It is a very beautiful and peaceful city where two-fifths of the population live in the surrounding suburbs. In the centre is a plaza, around which are clustered the main church, schools, government offices, and business establishments. The plaza is the centre of city life.

Silay was also boarding at the house in V. Rama, and of course we did many things together. One of our favourite recreational outings was to go to the cinema. Mama and Papa gave me some allowance, but I could only afford to see one movie per week. One week, Silay and I desperately wanted to watch *The Exorcist*, but we had already been to a movie on the Saturday. Our solution to the money crisis was to collect empty soft drink bottles and sell them. We collected three and a half sacks of empty bottles from Silay's grandparents and the other people in our boarding house. Silay contacted a buyer who was to come, pay, and collect the empty bottles. Our spirits were as high as Mount Everest. Three boys came. After negotiating and agreeing on the price of ₱10 pesos (about thirty Australian cents), the boys took the bottles and left. Silay sang out, "What about the money?" The older boy answered, "We are coming back." This was about eleven in the morning. We waited at the stairs . . . and waited . . . and waited, until six in the evening, and then we gave up, finally realising that we had been conned. We could not stop laughing—giggling at our stupidity. We should have got the money before giving them the bottles, but we had trusted the mongrels.

After finishing my first year at university, I decided to wait before continuing, as I was still uncertain about what I wanted to do. Then my sister Alma and her husband asked me to look after their firstborn son, who was expected any day. Having sympathy for my sister, who in the early months of her pregnancy had had a tumour removed, I reluctantly agreed.

I had not realized the enormity of the job ahead of me. It turned out that I was not only looking after my nephew but also doing what slaves used to do: scrubbing floors, washing clothes by hand, preparing meals three times a day, and carting five to eight litres of water a day up to the second floor where the family lived. It was also "voluntary"—I was not even paid an allowance to buy anything I needed!

It was hard labour, but because of my love for my nephew I stayed until the boy was one and a half years old; he was my life. I loved Nang Alma too, but unfortunately she gradually turned into the bully she had been in our childhood. Then one day my sister said some very upsetting words to me that made me decide to leave. She apologized but too late. I informed her that she had one month to find a replacement.

I loved my nephew so dearly; the thought of leaving him was breaking my heart. Then one night, when I was sleeping with him in my arms, I had a dream. The house was not screened, so during the night we used mosquito nets for protection. In my dream I saw the most magnificent red heart, the beautiful Sacred Heart of Jesus, beating directly in front of my eyes above the mosquito net. It stayed there for a minute or two, long enough for me to have a good look and appreciate it. It was the most remarkable heart I have seen in my life.

A month after my decision, I packed my bags and said goodbye to the family. I had a strange feeling toward my nephew, as if I had only just met him. It was very hard to explain. I should have collapsed when my sister put him into my arms to kiss goodbye, but in my mind was freedom. I was free! Looking back to my dream, I suppose it was a loving sign from God; He was showing me His Sacred Heart, a reassurance that I would be all right and that everything would be fine. Unfortunately, I didn't see the significance of it at that time.

After a number of years' break from school, I chose to return to the University of San Carlos to study Home Economics. After the first challenging and exciting year in this course, I began to see how important it was to me and, most importantly, to my students-to-be, their families, and the community in general.

In my last year I had a "practice house" for one semester, as part of the course. There were six girls, including me, in the House, called the Roof Garden, which was located on the sixth floor of the school building. We were looked after during the day, seven days a week, by a lecturer who was at the same time Matron of the House. She was exceptionally religious, grumpy, very strict, and a spinster. She made it clear to her residents that nobody was allowed off the premises of the House after 6.30 p.m. A security guard had the authority to stop us from leaving and bring us back to face the consequences. It was our matron's habit to come into our bedroom unannounced, at around 8.20 p.m., to do such things as check if our slippers were in the right place and facing the right direction, or tell us to lower the sound on our radios, as we all had miniature radios. (In the seventies television was a novelty which only the rich could afford.)

One particular night, we girls were just exploding with excess adrenalin after having been confined for about six weeks. Matron was surprised and favourably impressed when we were all suddenly very tired and retired to bed soon after dinner; she told us it would be a bonus in our assessments in eight weeks' time. Unusually she just barked, "Goodnight, everyone" and then she slipped out like a snake. We took this as our chance to get a breath of fresh air. I rang for a taxi and instructed the driver to park and wait a few metres from the main gate. Everything was going according to plan, and then we remembered the security guard! The other girls told me to go down and ask him to check the deliberately jammed front door. It was policy that no one was allowed to enter the Roof Garden after 7 p.m., so no carpenter could fix the door. If there was a problem, the security guard was the only one who could deal with it before morning. I went to fetch him, dressed in my pyjamas over my normal clothes, while the remaining five happy vegemites excitedly rode the elevator to the ground floor, and off we disappeared into thin air.

None of us thought about the risk of getting back *into* the house. We hadn't even planned for it. If we were caught, we risked suspension and no graduation—not to mention our parents' severe punishments! To avoid all this, we had to trick the poor security guard once more. Abbey, the bravest of us and a bit flirty, put on my pyjamas, which I'd hidden behind the fence, and confronted the guard. She pretended she was sleepwalking and asked where the toilet was. While she was "sleep-talking", the rest of us were in the elevator and on the way up to the house. We were very triumphant at our successful outing.

Before the end of the first semester, the university's student council organized a prom for the Faculty of Education, including all the major subjects, such as Home Economics. It was to be held at the Roof Garden. We six residents excitedly looked forward to the event, but only Abbey had an escort. Near the end of the prom, a residence friend and senior student, Inday, jokingly asked us if we were interested in meeting someone from abroad. She was holding a form asking for pen pals. She hadn't even finished explaining before we were signing up. My name was at the bottom of the list.

We parted at the end of the semester, in the year of 1978. We were all very happy and proud of our achievements. On my graduation night I received my Bachelor of Science in Education, majoring in Home Economics. However, I had very mixed feelings and was uncertain about my future. I was thirty-one years old.

Chapter 2

Six months after my graduation, I sat for the National Teacher's Board exam. The result was released in a year's time—I had passed! I was now a fully qualified, registered high school teacher in the Philippines. Unfortunately, jobs were very scarce in the seventies. To add misery and insult to those looking for work, it was the practice in our district to bribe any prospective employers. No matter how qualified and capable you were, without a "peace offering" you would always be at the bottom of the list of possible employees.

I became a teacher due to the influence of my late mother, Maria. She taught elementary school children from Grade 1 up before being promoted to Head Teacher in one of the schools in Aloguinsan. Mama was a down-to-earth teacher who preferred to teach Grade 1 children. She would say, "I experience joy and fulfilment in my career when a child manages to hold a pencil and write his or her name on a big piece of paper."

The school year in the Philippines begins in June and ends at the end of March. Before the school year began, I worked at the town council day care, with twenty pupils. Local election for the positions of mayor and councillors was approaching fast. The opposing party's candidate was a family friend, but my allegiance was to my employer, the current mayor. The mayor's wife knew of my loyalty, but was doubtful, and when she saw me and the opposition candidate's daughter walking together in the park, she confronted me and questioned my dependability. It was a very childish, unprofessional, and groundless accusation, and it caused me to resign from my job.

Purita, the opposition candidate's wife, offered to let me work for her in any of their shops, and I accepted the offer gratefully. A few weeks later, the postman handed four strange letters to Purita, which were addressed to me. They were in response to my name on the pen pal list I'd signed at university. There was one from America, two from Europe, and one from Australia. In spite of Purita's advice not to respond to all of them at once, I answered them straightaway. I was very excited! Letters from abroad—who could resist?

A gentleman from Broome, Australia, was my first choice. He had a house and an organ that he said he played occasionally. He was semi-retired and had money; he was a loner and divorced. My understanding of divorce was minimal, but I didn't care—he had a house!

Two days later, another letter arrived from Australia, from a man named John Lipsius. He was the only one of the five who explained in his letter about his life, where he lived and worked. He was at Savage River, a mining town in Tasmania, Australia, working at the mine, in administration. He lived in the single men's staff quarters.

Surprisingly, John was Purita's choice. She tried very hard to convince me to change my mind about the gentleman from Broome. However, my mind was made up—until he sent me another letter containing a scrap of material and a photo of a wedding dress, explaining that he'd spent a lot of money on the wedding dress for me as his future bride. I nearly fainted! It was hysterical, absolutely ridiculous! I'd never promised him anything and didn't really even know this man. Suddenly, I changed my mind about John.

After we had exchanged a few letters, John decided to take some holiday leave and come to the Philippines to meet me, sometime at the end of May. I reassured him that he would be in safe hands with me as his tour guide, although apparently I was not very convincing. According to John, it was just to be a friendly visit, unless meeting one another in person changed our minds. If we did hit it off, we would still have at least twenty happy years together, John wrote, as he was twenty five years older than me and already in his late fifties. His promise of twenty years was a bit off-track, as we have now been happily married for thirty-three years.

John was to arrive at lunchtime on a Saturday. I hadn't been game enough to tell my parents about him, mainly because he came from a different planet. I didn't know anything about Australia; obviously I hadn't been very good at geography. On Friday, Purita's daughter, together with her cousin, came to my home to ask if I could go to the city on the Saturday to do some purchasing for the shop, a job I normally did on Wednesdays. My Mama was a bit puzzled, but she agreed. So on Saturday morning, Purita and yours truly went very early to the city, picked up Silay's grandmother, Super, from V. Rama, and drove to the airport.

John was supposed to be arriving at 11 a.m. at Mactan Cebu International Airport, from Manila. Eleven o'clock passed, two sets of airbuses arrived, but there was no sign of John Lipsius. Purita and Super were afraid I was going to back out, and they treated me to lunch at the nicest restaurant in the airport. When I told them I was going back to Aloguinsan, they were shocked. "What are we going to do when he arrives? We cannot take this strange man to our homes! Our husbands would kill us!" They tried to convince me there was a reason he wasn't on the plane. Eventually Purita asked at one of the airline counters about John's flight; she discovered that it had been re-scheduled and would be arriving at 1.00 instead.

The airbus touched down on time. Nearly all the other passengers disembarked before Purita and Super at last saw John. They took his picture from a pocket, looked at the picture closely, and studied the approaching stranger. When they were certain, they sang out, "Mr John Lipsius?"

John, happy and relieved, said, "Yes." After the hugs and kisses, the other women introduced me to John. What an introduction! Then we took him to Hotel Magellan, only a few kilometres from V. Rama.

John had a wonderful time during his stay in Cebu City. We went everywhere with Super and her two gorgeous children: Sedrick, who was four, and Iris, who was two and a half years old. When Purita was in the city, she joined us also. I found John very likeable, genuine, honest, and very gentle in his manner. In other words, I liked him very much. Our age difference of twenty-five years did not bother me at all. It just didn't matter, as we both liked each other.

Time flew quickly, and John only had three weeks left of his seven-week holiday when we contemplated getting married. The big question was: How could we marry in two weeks' time? There were so many things to organize. We realized it would be a nightmare, but we were committed to each other and made up our minds that, with the help of friends and relatives, we would do anything to achieve it. We allocated various jobs: Alma would get the registrar; Nang Lena and Super would organize the celebrant and venue; Purita was to find the wedding dress and organize transport and witnesses, as well as being one of our witnesses. We had to have a civil wedding, as John was a Lutheran rather than a Roman Catholic as I was. John promised we would have a church wedding in Australia, as he was convinced that the Catholic Church in Australia allowed Catholics to marry those of other Christian denominations in their churches. The wedding was perfect, with only a few friends and family attending. It was the defining moment in my life, 21 June 1980. I was actually married to John! Mrs Teresita Pielago Lipsius. Wow!

My father and mother were pleased to have John as their son-in-law. "You could not have picked a better husband," Papa said, "but now I am sure you will have a happy life in Australia with John."

Purita lent us her house in Guadalupe to use until John left for Australia. His last week in Cebu was spent in organising my immigration papers for Australia.

One day we hailed a taxi to take us to the Australian Embassy in Makati, Manila. All the way there I tried to remember how to say "stop" in Tagalog, which is our national language. There are seven thousand islands in the Philippines, and each island has its own dialect. Tagalog is compulsory in all schools, but we don't all speak it every day, so for me Tagalog doesn't come naturally. I usually speak Visayan, as I grew up in the Visayan region of the Philippines. I would have been much better at speaking Tagalog if I had lived in Manila, even just for a few months, and had to use that language to communicate. However, I was so busy thinking of all the things to be done I panicked and told the driver to "para dong", which is Visayan for stop. The driver, who'd been talking in Tagalog all the way, answered in Visayan, and it turned out he came from Cebu. I felt like strangling him, as I'd been so anxious to get it right and be understood.

John left the Philippines for Australia, full of hopes, dreams, and excitement, to await my arrival in a month's time. We were assured by the people at the embassy that it would only take a month before I could join John in Australia. Unfortunately, it took two months.

Two weeks before my scheduled departure date, the government approval arrived, and then a second one arrived the following day, advising me to be ready to fly to Australia on 28 August. I found out later that John had sent enquiries to the Premier of Tasmania as well as the Immigration Department in Canberra, asking about the delay. No wonder I received two letters of approval.

A week before my departure, I visited my alma mater, the University of San Carlos, to use the university library, one of the oldest and biggest collections of books and references in the country. I wanted to find out more about the country I was moving to. I was sure John had said Australia, but I kept mixing it up with Austria. The accommodating, smiling lady at the counter was very willing to help me find some good information about where I was heading and what I could expect. She even provided me with a globe and a book called *Australia*. The word *Sydney* caught my eye. That was the place John was going to meet me.

The vast interior of Australia consists mainly of deserts and grasslands on which cattle and sheep graze, it read. My eyes were wide open and my heart sunk. Was that where I was going? The lady said, "I know what you are thinking. No, you won't be going to live in the desert, and you wouldn't be going to live with cattle and sheep, unless your husband is a farmer."

"Australia is huge," she continued. "I have been to Sydney a few times, because I have a brother who works as a doctor in one of Sydney's hospitals. And I have twice been to Tassie in the Christmas season. Oh, by the way, Tassie is a wonderful place to live. Tassie, as the locals call Tasmania, is an island. Yes, you are heading to a beautiful, clean, safe place in the world," she pronounced as she pointed to the map. "Australia is the only country that is also a continent. In area it ranks as the sixth-largest country and smallest continent. Australia is often referred to as 'down under' because it is situated in the southern hemisphere."

It was phenomenal. I just let her talk. She went on as though she were reading a bedtime story to a little girl. She was extraordinary, and I thought she must be a historian. It saved me from going to Austria instead of Australia, that's for sure. I learned all sorts of facts, such as: the name Australia comes from the Latin *australis*, meaning southern. Australia is a commonwealth and a dry and thinly populated country, but it is also one of the world's industrialized countries, with busy cities, modern factories, and highly productive farms and mines. Its two largest cities are Sydney and Melbourne, with Canberra, the national's capital, being only a short distance inland from these two cities. I also found out that it is famous for its vast open spaces, bright sunshine, enormous numbers of sheep and cattle, and plenty of unusual wildlife. I also found out that English is the official language and that Australians love outdoor sports and outdoor living. I discovered that it was once a British colony and that most Australians are of British ancestry. When people moved to Australia from Great Britain, they took with them many British customs, such as driving on the left side of the road, which was different to the Philippines, where we drive on the right.

"Tea is a popular drink in Australia, as it is in Britain," continued my fount of all knowledge. "Oh, and there is one important thing you should know about Australia's history. The first settlers were dark-skinned people who migrated from Asia thousands of years ago; today they are known as Aborigines. The Aborigines lived in Australia for at least forty thousand years before the first white settlers arrived. Since then the number of whites has increased and the number of Aborigines has declined. Today the majority of Australians are white."

A week before I flew to Manila, my Papa gave me two valuable treasures. One was a handful of dirt dug from our backyard and sealed in a plastic bag. Papa said, "Terrie, take this dirt with you to Australia. This dirt will help to ease the sad feelings about missing your family so much. Scatter it around your house or keep it as a keepsake." I have chosen the latter. When I received it my spirits were high; my feelings changed dramatically from sadness to enthusiasm, hope, and eagerness for my departure. The second treasure was a prayer in Visayan. Papa asked me to memorize it, saying, "Terrie, recite this prayer before leaving your house. You must say and make the sign of the cross after the prayer." I have been praying this prayer now for thirty-three years. So far it has worked. It is a very powerful prayer. I would encourage everyone to pray it; I am sure my late father would be happy to share his prayer. There is nothing to lose and everything to gain.

> *Because of the Blessed sign of the Holy Cross that cradled Jesus, protect me from all worries in my journey, and keep me safe from all danger. In the name of the Father, and of the Son, and of the Holy Spirit. Amen.*

It was time for me to leave Aloguinsan. I flew to Manila with Super and her children, who were bound for Hawaii. In Manila we stayed in the same hotel for a few days before saying goodbye and separating for good. My mind was preoccupied with the company of Super and her children, so there was not much time to think about my family back in Aloguinsan. Super's children were very close to me. They were gorgeous kids who have grown up into successful adults.

On the day of my departure from the Manila International Airport, there was no family to send me off, only two friends, Esing and Amy, both of whom resided in Manila. They stayed with me until my flight was called to board the plane. It was Philippine Airlines (PAL), the pride of the Philippines. My seat was located at a window about halfway up the aircraft. It was the longest flight I have experienced in my life, taking seven hours to arrive at the Sydney International Airport. For me it was like a lifetime. Reading or doing anything during that flight to occupy my mind was impossible. All I could do was watch the new moon and above it a lonely star glittering in the sky. It followed us from the time we took off from Manila until about half an hour before we landed in Sydney. We arrived very early on the sunny morning of 29 August 1980.

CHAPTER 3

Everything John had instructed me to do on arrival happened without incident. All my suitcases, two large ones and a carry-on, were already on a trolley. An announcement on the PA told all immigrants to head to the customs area for clearance.

When everything was cleared, we were directed to pass through the side exit out to the foyer/corridor where relatives and friends waited. To my surprise, John was not there. I waited, and the number of people dwindled, till this poor soul was the only creature left strolling along the corridor with a trolley full of suitcases. Somehow, though, I was not at all concerned that John might not turn up. I was absolutely confident that John was somewhere not far away.

An airport security guard became rather worried about the runaway or abandoned trolley in the corridor. He hurriedly walked over toward the trolley and took hold of it. I pulled it away from him. That was when he realized that there was someone pushing the trolley, that it hadn't just been abandoned. We were both startled, and it took him a few moments to recover. He apologized and explained that he hadn't seen me behind my pile of luggage. As I'm only five feet tall, I wasn't at all surprised. I confided to him that my husband hadn't turned up to collect me; his advice was to phone the number John had left me to contact in case of problems. However, my pride kicked in, and I thought that if John had changed his mind, why should I ring his nephew?

A middle-aged gentleman came by and said, "Luv, everythin' all right?" I looked around, thinking he must be talking to someone else by the name of Luv. He was staring at me, surprised, and he asked his question again. After I'd told him what had happened, he suggested I go to the Philippine Airlines counter and ask for the next flight back to the Philippines. At that moment I was neither sad nor contemplating going back home on the next available flight. The man was very nice, although I could hardly understand what he was talking about.

On my fourth lap along the corridor, for some reason, I looked over at the queue on my right. There, for a split second, I saw John's head looking at the nearly empty gate. I left my trolley, ran toward the gate, and tapped John on the shoulder. He turned around, amazed that it was me. He had waited and waited at the arrival gate but had never considered immigration clearance or the fact that immigrants might come through a different gate.

Now that we'd finally found one another, we proceeded to the Koala Hotel, located close to the central business district, where John had booked us for three nights. After leaving my bags in our room, we had breakfast, and then went sightseeing in Sydney. I started to feel the cold just looking through the hotel window, although it was a beautiful sunny day. Once outside, the cold just penetrated my bones, and my lips would not keep still. John did not notice this at all; his happiness and excitement were very obvious. Only when I asked him if we could go somewhere to buy some warm clothes did he finally realize how miserable I was.

We went to do some shopping for me, as I needed coats, jumpers, and cardigans, all warm clothing necessary for the cold weather. When I left Manila, the temperature had been 38 °C; when I arrived in Sydney, the temperature was only 12 °C. People said it was a mild morning, but I felt we were at the North Pole. I have never been there, but I have watched movies of Santa Claus with his reindeer year after year, and I've seen where he came from—the North Pole.

After our quick shopping trip, John took me to a restaurant near the Sydney Opera House for lunch, on a cruise around Sydney Harbour, and then to Circular Quay. It was there I encountered a very strange, stiff figure covered in blue paint from head to shoes; he just popped up from nowhere. I first noticed him when he was standing next to me on a milk crate, very stiff indeed, as stiff as the Statue of Liberty. "Excuse me sir, you put your crate on the handle of my handbag. Can you let go of it, please?" I asked, but the damn statue did not budge. People started coming, laughing, and putting money in the bucket in front of the milk crate. Japanese tourists started clicking their cameras. It was very unfortunate; it looked as if I were his assistant. My husband, also, was very amused. He told me it was an everyday occurrence in this place. He started clicking his camera as well, taking photos of me and the statue. I left my handbag and took shelter with my husband in the crowd, very upset. But because it was my first day in Australia, I pretended it was nothing. Thankfully, the stiff man only stayed for about ten minutes and then disappeared as quickly as lightning. Only when a lady handed me my bag did I realize the statue was gone.

After dinner that evening, we headed off to visit some of John's Lithuanian friends somewhere in a suburb, thirty minutes away by train. Wow! A train ride! This was a thrilling experience, as I'd never been on a train before. In my excitement I nearly forgot the freezing temperatures outside. Then reality sank in, and I chickened out. "C'mon Terrie, they are waiting for us. We have to go and see these people. They want to meet my wife," John said. I was betting it had been his idea.

So we boarded the train. Unfortunately, we got out at the wrong station; in other words, we got lost, stranded, on a freezing night. We went to a hotel's public bar to ask for directions and, if possible, to use the telephone. John told me that in Australia ladies weren't allowed in the bar, so he left me freezing outside the hotel foyer. My teeth were rattling as if they were doing drum rehearsals. It was dreadfully, horridly, terribly cold. So much for my wish to go somewhere where I would not perspire much! I'd rather have been in an oven to be roasted than rattling my teeth uncontrollably like this.

Also outside the hotel were some gentlemen, very jolly and conversing very loudly. Well, to put it mildly, they were overloaded with spirits. They could hardly stand up. After a few minutes, they noticed me standing not far from them. "Luv, if you—you—better go inside. You'll freeze to death here! Go to your bloody husband."

"Oh my! My husband is not bleeding is he?"

Everyone was laughing, choking, hardly able to utter a word. "Poor kitten! Your husband isn't bleeding; it's only bloody talk."

"Hey, Mayt! Lend your jacket to the lady," one middle-aged gentleman said. (I found out later that *Mayt* wasn't the name of a person but in everyday talk meant "friend".) "Mayt" refused to lend his jacket, claiming that it wasn't fit for a lady. Whatever he meant by "not fit for a lady", my first and lasting impression of Australia was the incredible friendliness and helpfulness of the people. No matter what state they're in, Australians have big hearts, and they are willing to help. That's very much in contrast to what I'd read in the seventies about Australia being a racist place. Welcome to Australia, Teresita. This is your ideal place to live.

When we finally got to their place, my husband's Lithuanian friends, John and Anticilli, were very pleased to meet me, and they seemed to be a nice couple. They actually lived in Launceston, the second-largest city in

Tasmania, after the capital of Hobart. They invited us to have dinner with them when we got to Launceston in a week's time, as they were heading back to Tassie in three days' time.

The following Saturday, 30 August, John's nephew, Walter, came with his two gorgeous girls to pick us up from the hotel where we had been staying. We had a quick tour around the Opera House and had some shopping time before we left Sydney. Walter took us to their home in Wahroonga to stay for a few days before we left for Tasmania. On the way to his home, he showed us some of the nice Sydney beaches. We arrived in time for dinner. Walter's wife, Pat was lovely. She welcomed me to their home and prepared a beautiful dinner; we chatted until very late in the night.

When we arrived in Launceston a few days later, we stayed at the Village Motel, not far from the Central Business District. We were welcomed by a beautiful sunny afternoon, but it was still bitingly cold. It was the second week in spring. The first thing I noticed were the gorgeous yellow flowers, called daffodils, in nearly every garden in Launceston. We stayed at the Village Motel for seven days before heading off on the final leg of the journey to Savage River.

Upon our arrival in Launceston, John rang the Lithuanian couple, John and Anticilli, whom we had met in Sydney. They happily invited us for a welcome dinner at their residence, which was just round the corner from where we were staying. I told John that I was so tired—all I wanted to do was rest! I wondered if he'd heard a word. He was so excited, looking forward to the dinner, and of course the company, and bursting to tell his Lithuanian friends about me and our wedding. He said his friends wouldn't accept no for an answer, so at seven o'clock, we went to the friends' place. We had a wonderful dinner with them, three other Lithuanians, and one Australian gentleman. They welcomed me as if I were a princess from an unknown place. I really enjoyed the company, and by the end of the evening I felt that I'd known them for a long time. Although they talked

Lithuanian most of the time, I didn't feel out of place. Our host, John, even taught me some Lithuanian phrases: *aciu labai*, pronounced *atchu laby*, meaning "thank you very much"; and *i sveikata*, pronounced *esrekata*, meaning "to your health".

At midnight I asked John if he could drive me back to hotel, as I was very tired, and then he could come back if he wanted. He agreed to drive me to the motel, but he went back to continue the conversation.

I found it difficult to settle down to sleep. Perhaps it was because of the strange place I was in, or because I was concerned about John, still in his friends' company. At 3 a.m. there was still no sign of John. There was a phone next to my bed; however, I didn't know the name of the street where John was or the couple's family name. Still in my dressing gown, I went outside to figure out which was the way to John's friends' place. It was a bit gusty, and the door slammed closed, locked, and left me standing there with no spare key!

I had no choice; the damn door was locked, and I couldn't get back into the room, so, my dressing gown tightly fastened, I started walking. The motel we were in was on the highway, but the traffic at three in the morning wasn't bad. Only one car, full of teenagers, passed. Then it reversed, stopped at my side, and a voice asked politely, "Good morning, lady. Are you all right? Where are you heading to?"

"Just around the corner. I am all right, thanks," I answered. The car went on very slowly and stopped at the corner with the engine still on, waiting until I turned the corner. The car only drove on when I had climbed up the steps of John's friends' place. They probably thought I was an escapee from an old people's home. Just as well they didn't call the police.

As I was too embarrassed to go inside, I simply knocked on the door, and then fled back to the motel. John followed me back and unlocked the door for us.

Over the next few days we did a lot of sightseeing, everywhere in the city and surrounding areas; we saw all the tourist spots. John was very relaxed, as he was very familiar with the place, and there were no hiccups. On our seventh day in Launceston, it was time for us to head off to Savage River. We spent the whole morning shopping for groceries, crockery, and cutlery. Friends of John's advised him to drive back to Savage River at night, which for some reason they thought would assist me in not getting carsick and therefore avoid getting a bad first impression of the place. John agreed.

Unfortunately, after lunch John looked exhausted and complained of a slight headache. He took two Panadol tablets and lay down, but he developed a very high temperature. He was shivered badly and asking for more blankets, so we decided to go to the hospital. The doctor advised him to stay in the hospital for a few days until his fever subsided. However, John was worried about me being alone in the motel, so he asked the nurse if he could stay in the motel instead of the hospital. Luckily they agreed. They gave us all the prescribed medicines, the hospital's emergency numbers, instructions for sponge bathing, and so on. It was another six days before John was well enough to travel.

We eventually left Launceston late one afternoon, hoping to be in Savage River by 10 p.m. When we got to the town called Waratah, in the north-west, my tummy began to complain so badly that I had to open the window for some fresh air. It did not help. The freezing wind that hit my face prompted me to close the window up again. My husband kept saying, "It won't be long. Another half hour and we'll be there."

Half an hour? It seemed a lifetime to me, but I never said a word. It was not only the length of travelling time but the climbing up and up and up on an endless winding road. Eventually I asked John, "How much higher are we going to climb? It looks like it is only a five-cent fare to Heaven." I didn't even get to finish my sentence; John had to stop the car to let me be violently sick. It was only a few minutes after this that

I saw lights. I couldn't believe my eyes! First there were just a few lights on the streets, then more lights appeared, and further up, a very well-lit place—a beautiful place, like paradise—came into view. The lit scene was a very welcome sight after two hours of driving in inky-black darkness on winding roads.

John slowly turned off to Pieman Place, which looked like an army barracks, parked in front of number 18, and said, "Welcome to your new home." He explained that married couples without children stayed in flats; couples with children were allowed a three bedroom house. I had a hard time with the word *flat*. Another word added to my vocabulary: *mayt*, *luv*, and now, *flat*. I was later informed that it meant apartment.

Inside the flat it was very cosy. Everything we needed was there—except curtains. All the windows were bare, although all you could see in the pitch black outside was the distant well-lit hydro plant. The first thing John did was to turn the oil heater on full. Can you imagine a wet bird wanting to warm and dry its feathers? Well, that's how I was. I stood with my behind right in front of the heater, gradually warming up. John wanted to show me around, but it was impossible for him to peel me off the heater.

The next morning the sun was shining brightly. It was the first week in October, the middle of spring. Out the back of our flat there were tall trees and green bushes as far as my eyes could see, and there were yellow flowers everywhere. One thing I noticed, though, was that there was not a single soul walking along the street. Back home in the Philippines, in Aloguinsan in particular, there is something wrong when you cannot see people moving and walking in the middle of the streets. *Strange place*, I thought.

After breakfast, someone knocked at the door. It was our next-door neighbours from flat number 19, a middle-aged couple without children. They were our first visitors; they wanted to make themselves known to me. This beautiful couple, Sid and Gale, tried their utmost to make me feel welcome and comfortable. They looked after me as if I were their own daughter.

Gale worked at the hotel as an assistant chef; Sid was a fitter in the mine. Gale taught me how to prepare Australian foods and even bought a culinary book for me to practice some Australian recipes. Nearly all ingredients were the same as in the Philippines; the only difference was the preparation and cooking. Filipinos are used to cutting and dicing the meat, but our staple is rice, unlike the Australian potatoes and bread.

On 15 October I had my first birthday in a foreign country. Gale and Sid organized a party for me; they made some tasty nibbles, savouries, main courses, and desserts. The birthday cake was the centre of attraction. Gale had meticulously decorated it with edible flowers. The party was very successful, allowing me to meet a few people. Everyone enjoyed the night, thanks to Gale's efforts. The people at Savage River were very welcoming, accommodating, helpful, and exceptionally friendly. Straightaway I felt a sense of acceptance and community. I was very grateful that they accepted me into their community.

Savage River mine, owned by a Canadian company, was one of the largest mines in Tasmania; it produced iron ore. The minerals were pumped in slurry form through a pipeline, for about fifty kilometres, to a palletizer plant located at Port Latta. From here they were loaded onto bulk carriers for export to other countries. From the eighties to the nineties, Savage River was a town with a population of about fifteen hundred. It had its own hospital, gym, large supermarket, tennis court, heated swimming pool, cricket ground, church, petrol station, police station, chemist, two gift shops, three banks, and a district school with about seven hundred students. A greengrocer came every Wednesday to deliver and sell fresh produce, and a fruit-juice van came twice a week. The place catered for everything one needed; it was like a little city.

My first week in Savage River was a bit daunting. John was always at work. I tried to practice the recipes and learn how to use the utensils, as some were a bit strange. Then I would happily put my experiment on the dinner table. John said, "This was delicious. Very tasty. Oh! I invited some friends and the town manager to have dinner with us. Just a simple meal. Won't be any problem, will it?"

Yes, I thought, *it is very easy for you to say*, but I never said it aloud. The trouble was I was still shy with my husband. I could not voice my ideas or opinions and tried very hard not to offend him. Mama would say the first months are a period of adjustment. They certainly were for me.

One day when John was at work, I cooked rice for the first time in my Australian life. It was lovely to have rice at last. The next morning, as usual, he got up before me. He called to me, sounding scared and pointing at two grains of swollen rice that had accidently remained in the sink overnight. He thought they were maggots. My tears dribbled. I was very upset and humiliated—my rice turned into maggots!

Another afternoon we went for a good look around the township, where we met some nice people, and then went to the supermarket. Our last stop was the pub. John was with a few of his workmates, drinking beer in the bar, while I had a coffee in the lounge. After about an hour, I went to the bar and asked John if we could go home. The gentlemen in the bar were surprised, because nobody—nobody—came to the bar asking their husbands to go home. They wouldn't tolerate that habit, John explained when we were driving home. Well, bad luck! I'd had enough, and I wanted to go home.

When John was at work, I would close all my curtains, unhook the telephone from the cradle, and pretend that nobody was home. I avoided having visitors for coffee or morning tea invitations. A knock at the door or the ringing of the phone petrified me. John tried to encourage me to talk to people, in order to get rid of what he called the chip on my shoulder.

Although the Filipino's second language is English, like Tagalog, it is not used in everyday conversation. Intonation, pronunciation, and even spelling are all Americanized. All our references and textbooks are from the United States. Therefore, it wasn't surprising that I would pronounce words very differently to Australians. One day a lady friend invited me to go for a walk, saying, "If we have time, we'll call in to see the baby." She pronounced it as *bye-be*. In my simple understanding, we were going for a swim at the bay! The thing that worried me most was that even when people swallowed or murdered the words, other people still understood what they were talking about. Every time a person approached me, I froze.

Every month in Savage River, a newsletter was printed to let residents know about things happening in the community. A headline in the November issue was Staff Christmas Dinner. John explained that the Christmas dinner hosted by the mining company was not just for mining personnel but also for all white-collar workers in Savage River, including the people who worked at the school, banks, and supermarket.

When December came around, I was already prepared—excited, but also apprehensive about attending this function. At the dinner party it happened that the school's secretary was at our table. The others at our table were very curious about me. Well, I was not surprised, as I must have been the first coloured creature crawling around Savage River. Some were fascinated by my accent, and some were envious of my colour. Maybe they were joking, or perhaps it was my beautiful off-the-shoulder gown that Gale had made for me. Gale was a very good seamstress; she was a lady of many talents. The school's secretary asked me about my country, about the area of the Philippines I came from, whether we spoke/understood English—tell-me-about-yourself sort of thing. I boasted about my qualification, telling them that I had recently graduated with a Bachelor of Education, majoring in Home Economics.

CHAPTER 4

The first school term for all public schools in Tasmania began in the second week of February, 1981. On the Thursday in the third week of February, the Savage River School secretary and principal came to our flat, introduced themselves, and asked if I was interested in teaching at their school. My answer was a yes, but probably in five years' time, after getting acquainted with the environment and the people of my new country.

For some reason, the headmaster didn't take any notice of what I had said, whether he hadn't understood my accent or just hadn't heard what I'd said. He asked about my diploma. I thought they were doing some type of census of new arrivals, so I answered all their questions and gave them my credentials. The headmaster had copies of all the important papers sent to the Education Department. After a short conversation with the school secretary, he turned to me and asked me, "Would you like to start teaching tomorrow, Friday?"

I gave a resounding, No! as an answer. I had never been to the school and didn't even know where it was. I was a fresh graduate from a Philippines university, with no teaching experience and no time to familiarize myself with what had been taught during the previous two weeks. I was completely unprepared to be the only Home Economics teacher, without even a teacher's aide.

However, because he was desperate to fill the position, the Principal ignored my excuses. Instead, he handed me a set of school keys and organized for the Vice-Principal to collect me the following day, so I could observe a Grade 7 Home Economics class.

The next day, the Vice-Principal took me to the class, where they were having a theory lesson, and left me to the mercy of these unknown people. I sat quietly next to the door, and I heard a few boys whisper to one another, "We have an Asian classmate."

At the end of the lesson, the teacher, Mrs Clements, introduced herself to me and begged me to accept the job, as she was desperate to join her family in Sydney. Her family had already moved to Sydney, but because a replacement teacher had not been found, Mrs Clements had stayed behind.

So I ended up accepting the offer, although with some fear and uncertainty! I agreed to begin teaching on the Monday, but only for one term, until they could find a more permanent replacement.

Mrs Clements showed me six crates of folders in her little office, which were the previous year's students' records, resources, recipes, and lesson plans for Grades 7 to 10. Mrs Clements told me that all the information I required was in those folders. There were four classes each of year 7 and 8 students, three classes of year 9s, and two of year 10 students. I would be teaching both cooking and sewing, as well as being the Home Economics coordinator and having to purchase all necessary supplies.

Mrs Clements continued, "The Grade 7 classes will have cooking on the last two periods on Monday afternoon. They are making apple crumble. I have done the demo (demonstration) during their single lesson. The kids are good and will know what to do, although you have to keep an eye on each of them. They'll be fine.

"The pantry is half-full, good for a week's consumption. The cleaners will help you. Oh! By the way, period three and four after recess on Monday, you'll need to do a demo, for year eights, of a shepherd's pie. The recipe is in the year eight's cooking folder. Oh, I am sorry. But you'll be fine."

As Mrs Clements kept talking, I did not say a word. It was a nightmare! I thought for a moment, *Where am I? Am I on Planet Earth?* My mouth was open all the time, but no words came out. I wanted to say something, but I was totally tongue-tied.

"Good luck, Terrie. Everything will be fine." said Mrs Clements. After giving me a tour of the sewing room, pantry, and laundry room, she handed me the keys, and I left. John and I were heading off to Hobart to attend a Lithuanian festival for the weekend.

There was no enjoyment for me at the Lithuanian festivities. My brain was tortured as my hands were busy writing Monday's lesson plans. My eyes were busy reading the recipes and studying the step-by-step procedure, for I had never heard of shepherd's pie before. Luckily, almost all the ingredients were familiar to me, apart from some of the herbs and spices. On the Sunday, I phoned from Hobart for some more information and instructions for Monday. Unfortunately Mrs Clements had already left. John and I left Hobart on Sunday afternoon, arriving back in Savage River very late at night. Luckily I didn't have to prepare dinner, as we had stopped on the way home for something to eat.

The dreaded Monday came. I got up very early, scanned the lessons for the first two periods, and off I went. John drove me to the school on his way to work. He was nervous, but confident that I could do it. "Good luck, my girl. I know you can do it," he said.

Mr Julius Kearon, the principal of the school, met and welcomed me at the car park. Then took me to the staff room and introduced me to all the other staff. As you can imagine, my body was present, but my spirit was nowhere to be found. There I was, at a strange place, among strange people, in a strange environment, and having to learn a strange school routine. I was a complete stranger.

I was very shy, with an inferiority complex, and I was afraid of racial discrimination, particularly because I had difficulty with the language. I was also concerned that my teaching standards wouldn't meet the school's expectations. I just had to trust that with the knowledge gained during my studies and training as a teacher, and with some advice and help from my new colleagues, I would be able to carry out my job satisfactorily. Thankfully, once I began teaching, my fear and uncertainty were quickly forgotten. Instead, my attention was focused on teaching and the students' learning progress.

My first morning began with class-teacher period. I introduced myself and emphasized that I would only be their teacher till the end of the first term. Whilst I called names to check attendance, the students whispered to each other and giggled. I thought, *Oh my! I must have said something funny that made them laugh.* During that entire dreadful Monday—or, as the locals would say, "bloody miserable day"—when I called out the names I would get the same reaction. Nobody would tell me what it was all about or what was going on. The more I asked, the more they giggled. That was the order of the day for a whole. Except at the beginning, I didn't see the Principal. He purposely left me alone. He didn't want to get me nervous because of his presence, he explained later.

At the end of the day, one brave girl introduced herself and said her name was Pauline. She said, "You pronounced my name funny. You said *Pawleen.*"

I replied, "That is your name, isn't it?"

"Yes," she said, "but it is pronounced *Poleen*." Or something like that. Other students then came forward and said that I had mispronounced their names also.

"Ah! That's why every time I called your names you giggled?" A big nod and Yes! To avoid more clowning the following day, I spent nearly the whole night rehearsing their names.

The next day, before calling their names, I warned the students, "Please correct me and forgive me if I mispronounce your name. You know I am from a different planet. The way your name is spelled is the way I read and pronounce it." The atmosphere changed; the students relaxed and laughed at my joke. I felt they appreciated my truthfulness. From then on, the students started to feel comfortable; correcting me when they thought my pronunciation was funny. They started dropping by at my classroom to say hello or good morning. Bingo! I had broken the ice.

It was my first cooking lesson with the Grade 8 class on the Wednesday, the shepherd's pie. One of the boys sang out, "Mrs Lipsius, can you please come and check my spuds?"

My heart started to beat faster, faster than any jet plane. *"Spuds?" What the hell is that?* I wondered. There had been no spuds mentioned in their ingredients, or had I given them the wrong recipe? I deliberately made myself busy with someone else's cooking, to avoid confrontation with the blooming "spuds". Eventually I went over to the boy to find out about these things called spuds—they were potatoes! I could hardly see the potatoes, anyway; they were all mushy, well overcooked. "Next time when you call out for help, make sure you say the proper name for things, in plain English. You know pretty well I came from a different planet, so have mercy on me." Everyone laughed and giggled; they asked what planet I came from. The spuds episode was actually a blessing.

One week passed well. Heavens knows how I did it, but I did it! I survived the first daunting week. The Principal was pleased and full of praise. Actually, most of the school's staff was very supportive. I was not certain about my strengths and weaknesses as a teacher, but I felt that I had managed successfully so far. It was a very daunting experience for the start of my teaching career.

The students at Savage River District High School were very well disciplined and well behaved, but as any teacher will know, there is always a black sheep in a herd. Luckily, I got along well with students. It seemed that they liked me as much as I liked them, which was really a huge bonus for me as a complete stranger in paradise. The good thing was that I did love the company of children, and the rapport between me and the students was incredible.

The North West branch of the Home Economics Association of Tasmania was scheduled to hold their term meeting at Penguin, a beautiful town on the north-west coast of Tasmania. The President of the Association very kindly officially invited me to this meeting, offered some professional help if needed, and supplied me with some instruction. The main purpose was to introduce me to the other Home Economics teachers in the area. It would do me good and make me feel more at ease to know that I wasn't alone and that there were others there ready to help. In fact, they encouraged me to join the Association. I jumped at the offer and enrolled. Mrs Pat Coy, who was President of the Association at that time, wrote a letter to Mr Kearon, the Principal, asking if she could come officially to observe my Home Economics classes.

During the first three weeks of my time at the school, one of the male staff brought his shirt to the Home Arts room and asked me to mend it for him, as there were some buttons missing. So at lunch break, instead of having my lunch, I was busy attaching buttons to the shirt. A week later, the same gentleman brought his dirty, muddy running shoes to me and asked me to clean them for him. Not a if-you-don't-mind-doing-this-for-me sort of thing, but said in a way which indicated he expected me to do it. Back home in Aloguinsan, although we were not well off, most of the time we had a domestic helper to do things like clean shoes. I found it a bit strange that this man would ask me, but when you are an alien on a different planet, you tend to do things to please to people, especially when you think it might actually be part of your job.

However, when I mentioned it to John at dinner, he fumed with anger. "Extracurricular activities such as mending and cleaning dirty, rotten, filthy shoes are not your job and will *never* be a part of your job as a Home Arts teacher," John furiously barked. "He is manipulating you, taking advantage of you because you are new in town and new in the workforce. He is a bully!" It took me quite a while to calm John down. I begged him not confront the gentleman. I thought it was partly my fault, because I was so ignorant of expectations and lacked experience in everything at work. I promised it wouldn't happen again.

Two weeks before the end of the first term, the Principal handed me the contract for the second and third terms, saying, "This means you are going to finish the whole school year, Mrs Lipsius." Apart from the classes I already had, two extra Grade 6 classes had been added to my load, beginning in second term.

One weekend John and I decided not to go anywhere; instead I would do some work at school. Not far from the cooking room's main door there was an annex, which was very dark. No light could get in, as black tape sealed all the windows and the glass in the door. Any small cracks were heavily covered with black tape. *Wow!* This was one strange room, like a haunted one. The room was not only dark, it was dirty. Wet cloth lay everywhere, and newspapers were scattered on the floor. So I set aside my half-day for cleaning and clearing this room. I pulled off all the black tape, wiped all the windows and doors, cleaned the rugs, put the newspapers into the bin, and swept the floors until the room looked wonderfully, immaculately clean. I was very proud of myself and thought I'd done a marvellous job. I couldn't wait to tell the cleaners what I'd done over the weekend, though I was still puzzled and could not figure out why all the black tape had been over everything.

Monday came, and as usual, I was an early bird at school. I heard footsteps click-clacking on the wooden corridor; because it was very early in the morning, the sound of the heavy shoes seemed extra loud, echoing along the whole passage. The footsteps stopped in front of the annex room. It was a man by the sound of it, and he was very irritated. "What the hell is going on?" he uttered angrily, and so on and so forth. I was pretty sure he was swearing, but fortunately it was in English, so I could not comprehend a word, anyway.

Then another male voice said, "Good heavens!"

I froze. *Oh, help!* I realized I'd done something terrible to the annex room—but what? All I had done was to clean a very dirty room. *Oh, Teresita! What have you done this time that has made the men so cross?* To tell the gospel truth, my legs and hands were shaking like jelly as I waited for the men to storm into the kitchen and ask for explanations. I was as scared as a rabbit out of its burrow. I was already rehearsing what to say; I waited and waited and waited and waited, but they never came. The end of the day came, and nobody confronted me about what had happened to the annex room. I felt a bit guilty about what I had done, though I had thought I'd been doing the right thing. But I was so scared, as the tone and language of the two men had sounded so angry—"pissed off", as the locals would say.

At the end of the year I asked one of the staff about the annex room. They explained that it was the dark room, used for photography. *Oh, help!* How could I have known it was a photography room? Nobody had mentioned anything to me about the strange room next door. As it was long past, I hoped those two men had forgiven me for the incident. It was not entirely my fault; I had been told to occasionally help the cleaners if I had any spare time. Well, that was exactly what I had done.

Toward the end of that year, there was a fuss about "Hawthorn". Nearly all the school staff were wearing yellow ribbons on their chests. I, without asking—there was no point, because I rarely understood what they were doing or talking about—just pinned a yellow ribbon on my top and went everywhere with it. All the students were whispering that Mrs Lipsius was a "Hawthorn supporter". At the end of the day I asked one of the other staff, "What is Hawthorn?" They told me they barracked for a football team called Hawthorn, which was going to play over the weekend.

It is amazing how time flies if you are incredibly busy. It felt like only yesterday that I had experienced my daunting first day, first week, and first month of my teaching career. Now it was time to bid goodbye to the Grade 10 students, my first graduates, the *most* beautiful, helpful, understanding students I have met in my life. They learned from me, but I learned more from them. The parting was very emotional. I hid from them so I wouldn't have to take part in the photo shoots. The students looked everywhere for me, even asking John where I was; they didn't want to have their photos taken unless I was with them. How incredible! They were my 1981 graduating class.

At the end of the 1981 school year, the Principal informed me of and congratulated me on an appointment for the following school year, 1982. My mouth was open, but not a word came out. I was very overwhelmed. I must have done something good to please the school and staff.

During the end-of-year dinner that year, everyone congratulated me on my incredible braveness, courage, and perseverance. The Principal's comments and Senior Master's end-of-year evaluation show it all. The Principal's comments are from 1981, and the Senior Master's from 1982.

Enthusiasm for teaching: (P) Very enthusiastic about being a teacher and about teaching Home Arts. It is unfortunate that because her timetable is completely taken up with secondary Home Arts she is unable to involve herself in other areas of the school or in other subjects. **(SM)** Very enthusiastic, highlighted by dedication, keenness to start early, quality/quantity of planning.

Ability to motivate pupils: (P) This is good in Grades 9 and 10. She has not always been as successful with Grades 7 and 8. **(SM)** Satisfactory. More successful with Grade 7 and 8 pupils.

Quality of preparation and planning: (P) This has always been most thorough. She is always well prepared for the day's teaching. **(SM)** Very organized and well thought through. Always written in advance. Cooking costed through in advance.

Control and discipline of classes: (P) She has tended to accept too much rudeness and bad manners from some pupils. The working atmosphere tends to be a bit too easy-going. This latter point has led to some students running up quite high debts in connection with materials that have been supplied for cookery. **(SM)** Has improved—Terrie now takes a firmer line of control. Some instances of bad manners (e.g., students interrupting) still apparent.

Rapport with the students: (P) This is generally good. This is evidenced by tendency for some pupils to treat the Home Arts room a bit like a drop-in centre. **(SM)** Good.

Willingness to accept and act on advice: (P) She is very keen to improve her performance as a teacher, and she seeks advice to help her achieve this. **(SM)** Very willing.

Variety, range, and effectiveness of class management techniques: **(P)** Initially there was too much theory taught in Grades 7 and 8, but this has been modified to a largely practical course. **(SM)** Rather more movement around the classroom during practical classes would assist with class management.

Personal qualities: (P) Punctuality and reliability are both very good except for the bus-duty roster. Her relationship with the rest of the staff is very good. She has a conscientious approach to her work. She is always keen to know what correct procedures are, and she tries to follow them. **(SM)** Very reliable and loyal to the staff and school. Relates well with children, keen to teach and develop as a teacher. Willing to accept advice. Respected by staff.

Ability to sustain effort: (P) Terrie works very hard, continuously, in and out of school hours, planning and preparing for lessons. **(SM)** Terrie starts work very early and stays late. Doesn't appear to fatigue as a term develops. Has continued to look for improvement and self-development.

Appearance: (P) She is always neatly and smartly presented. She sets a high standard as an example to her students. **(SM)** Of a consistently high standard. Sets example to students.

Marking and checking of work: (P) She has not enforced the completion of set work, particularly assignments. It seems that she is making an attempt to correct this. Assessment of class work is quite satisfactory. **(SM)** Satisfactory records kept. Work assessed when completed. Terrie now works at a more reasonable level.

Concern for and interest in the well-being of students and their progress: **(P)** Terrie has very great concern for her students, especially those in Grades 9 and 10. **(SM)** Terrie displays much concern for the well-being of students in her care. She is concerned for their education.

Terrie Lipsius

Confidentiality regarding the professional side of school: (P) Good.
(SM) Very professional in approach.

There you are—judging by the Principal's and Senior Master's comments, it seems I was heading in the right direction. I would like to comment about the bus duty. I did not do bus duty for the whole year of 1981, not because of negligence or laziness, but because I didn't understand what bus duty meant. Nobody ever told me off about my bus duty, but obviously there were some good Samaritans who did my bus duty for me and never mentioned it to me. Not until the end-of-the-school-year functions did some teachers ask me jokingly to compensate them for their labour in religiously doing my bus duty twice a week.

The Savage River District High School staff were friendly, extremely helpful, and easy to get on with. I suppose there were one or two unhappy souls, but I never met them. I had a ball, the most wonderful experience of my life. I owe my life to each one of them, from the Groundsman to the Principal. They were an incredible bunch of people. I have missed those lovely years at SRDHS. I have missed all those beautiful staff. I would like to say a heartfelt thank you to all of you, for without your help and advice I would never have been able to survive.

I have the privilege of including a reference letter from my Principal, which I requested in the year 2003.

To whom it may concern re: Mrs Teresita Lipsius

I was Principal of Savage River District High School from 1981 to 1983 inclusive. Mrs Lipsius was a teacher at the school during 1981 and 1982. She had a temporary appointment and in 1983 she was replaced by a teacher who had recently completed her teacher training in Tasmania.

When I approached Mrs Lipsius early in 1981 to enquire if she was able and willing to take up a teaching position at my school, she had only recently completed her teacher training overseas, and she was a recent immigrant into Australia. She was thus a beginning teacher in every sense of the words. She had much to learn, but she was very keen to improve her performance as a teacher, and she sought advice to help her achieve this. She acted on advice she received. The fact that her temporary appointment was continued for two years is testimony that I was satisfied with her performance. It was through no action of mine that she was replaced in 1983.

I have lived in Deloraine since 1984, but the friendship between Mr and Mrs Lipsius and me and my wife has continued since that time. I have made the comments which follow from notes I made in 1981 and notes made by a senior member of my staff in 1982.

Mrs Lipsius was very enthusiastic about being a teacher and teaching what was then known as Home Arts. Her lesson preparation was very thorough, and she was always prepared for the day's teaching. She was a hard and conscientious worker. As a result, she proved to be successful at motivating her pupils. Mrs Lipsius had a good rapport with her students, and she demonstrated great care and concern for them. Generally speaking, her teaching was very effective, but this effectiveness was sometimes compromised by the rather easy-going atmosphere which pervaded her lessons.

Mrs Lipsius was very punctual, reliable, and well presented, and she had a very good relationship with the other staff members. She had a very professional approach to her work.

(SIGNED)

Julius Kearon

Chapter 5

On 4 April, 1981, exactly ten months after I had arrived in Savage River, John and I celebrated our church wedding in the Church of Apostles, in Launceston. John had promised before our civil wedding in the Philippines that we would have a church wedding in Australia. He had believed that Australian Catholic churches did marry Catholics to Christians from different denominations, and he had been right. The priest of the Church of Apostles was happy to marry us. Actually, we only wanted a Church blessing of our civil wedding.

Thirty guests attended, mostly John's friends and colleagues from Savage River and Stanley and his Lithuanian friends from Launceston. Mr John Krutulis played the wedding march on the church organ while John and I walked down the aisle to the waiting priest at the altar. I wore a beautiful apricot-coloured wedding dress with a matching hat, which had been made by my dearest friend, Mrs Gale Brown. It was a simple, but very solemn, wedding. It was rather emotional for me, though, as there were no relatives of mine present at this important moment of my life.

From the church, we headed to a reception at the Olde Tudor Inn, a few kilometres outside the Launceston CBD, where we had booked in for a couple of days. We received a congratulatory telegram from Mama and Papa, as well as from John's nephew and niece from Sydney, who hadn't been able to come because they were in Europe at that time.

A month after our second wedding, and eleven months after I had arrived in Savage River, I received an official visit from two police officers from the neighbouring town of Waratah, to ask if I would like to become an Australian citizen. The explained the benefits and privileges that would come with being an Australian citizen. Although I loved my new country very much, I felt that I was not quite ready to become an Australian, so I asked if it was possible to have a dual citizenship. The officer replied, "Yes, of course. However, sometimes there are complications, like having to pay taxes in Australia and the Philippines at the same time, or Australia might deny you some of the privileges that would otherwise be available to you." After considering what I had been told, I decided to change my Philippine citizenship to an Australian one. It was arranged that I would have my naturalization ceremony at the Council Chambers in Waratah, because I did not want to attend the ceremonies in either Launceston or Hobart with the rest of the migrants. I preferred to have a quiet, but solemn, service conducted by the Warden of Waratah and an Immigration Department official from Launceston. And so, on 10 July 1981, I officially became an Australian citizen. I have never looked back nor regretted my decision; I enjoy living in Australia and being a citizen of my adopted country.

During the school term break, John and I had a chance to wander around Savage River and the surrounding areas. Most important for me was to find where the local Catholic Church was. It turned out that there was no Catholic Church in the area, which was a bit disappointing. Mass for the Catholic community was celebrated by a priest from Rosebery every third Sunday of the month, in the Savage

River Community Church, which was used in turn by all the Christian denominations. The Savage River Community Coordinator informed me that they were looking for volunteers to clean the church once a month before the scheduled service.

There were four of us who volunteered: a couple from Luina, me, and Mrs Adam, who lived just across from the church building. For some reason, the altar was very bare; there were no pictures, no cross, nothing which would tell me that I was actually inside a church. Anyway, it was my habit to bring flowers to the church every Sunday. Whether there was a Mass or not, I would arrange some flowers neatly in a vase on the altar/table. My life without a place to worship is empty; something is missing. Luckily, all the volunteers were given keys to the building, and so I could go there anytime I wanted to do something.

Toward the end of first term of 1982, some Sisters of Mercy (nuns) from the Hobart Diocese stayed at the Community Church in Savage River for a few weeks. They were looking for volunteers to teach catechism for a period of eight weeks, beginning at the middle of second term and running until the second week in October. There were to be two groups of children: the First Communicants, or Grade 7 children preparing for their first Holy Communion, and Confirmation, the Grade 8 children preparing to be confirmed.

On their first Saturday, I took in fresh-cut flowers to the Community Church and arranged them beautifully in a vase. I wasn't even aware that some people were staying there. The Sisters were astonished, wondering who had put flowers on the altar. They enquired around and after discovering that it was me, they arranged to meet me in order to discuss the possibility of my teaching the children catechism.

There were to be ten Grade 7 students preparing for Holy Communion, every Monday and Wednesday afternoon at the Community Church, and eight Grade 8 students preparing for Confirmation every Tuesday and Thursday afternoon straight after school. The Sisters reassured me that guidelines would be provided and sent to me within two weeks so that I could familiarize myself and study the contents.

What am I doing teaching the catechism? I wondered. I was a devoted Roman Catholic, but I had never intended to be a nun or anything like that. To tell you the truth, during my university days I had had difficulty getting a passing mark for my theology subjects. Religion in secondary schools and Theology in the universities were compulsory subjects in all Catholic schools in the Philippines. I failed them. My parents, as you can imagine, were furious when they were notified that their daughter couldn't graduate unless she passed all her Theology subjects. I love God, I respect God, I try to be a good person, but reading, studying and interpreting the Bible is just not my cup of tea.

It's probably due to a childhood experience; my uncle was, of course, born and brought up as a Catholic by Catholic parents. Then, when he had his own family, he became a "Saturday Adventist". I thought that because nearly every time I saw my uncle he was carrying and often reading his Bible, that maybe that could happen to me. What if I became the same as my uncle and changed my religion? Maybe remembering my uncle was the reason I avoided the Bible whenever possible. However, I had no choice but to study it at school. Miraculously, at the end of my fourth year, I did manage to pass all my Theology subjects. Don't ask me how I did it, but I did!

Now I was about to teach the catechism. Oh, Heaven help me! I knew there were twelve Apostles of Christ. That was easy, "a piece of cake" as the locals would say—but who were they? The Sunday Missal Book was handy. The trouble was there were few familiar names. If I added them up, there would be eighteen, six more than the required number of apostles! So during the school holidays I was forced to study the Bible. I began using it as my main reference, supplemented by the resources sent to me by the Sisters of Mercy.

Before beginning, we had a get-together with the parents involved as well as our parish priest. Savage River belonged to the West Coast Parish of Rosebery, a neighbouring mining town. The priest came once a month to say Mass for the Catholic community. I needed to meet the priest, the parents, and the children involved and to get their support; this would be crucial for a successful outcome for the children. Parents, relatives, and carers all pledged to spend time to help coach their children with their homework. The response was overwhelming.

It was proposed that the Holy Eucharist and Confirmation would be held on the same Sunday, toward the end of second term. Parents were asked to dress their children in special clothes, if possible. The girls were to wear white dresses with matching white veils and the boys black trousers with white shirts. To my surprise, the parents were delighted with the idea of having their children wear the traditional black-and-white attire for this very special occasion. The children looked lovely, and the realization of my dream was just unbelievable.

In October 1981 John and I sent a letter inviting my Mama and Papa to come and visit us in Australia. John boastingly added, "You will see how your daughter lives: her new lifestyle and how well she's adjusted at her new home, even though it hasn't even been a year since she arrived in Savage River." In the letter we told my parents that their return tickets had already been purchased. All they needed to do was to find a travel agent to process their visas. A month after we sent this letter to them we had an answer, strangely, from Mama only, saying, "Regrettably, your Papa will not be able to come to Australia in December, as it is the peak season for milk fish fry. It is the harvesting time for the matured milk fish, and your father has to be present to supervise the fry catcher."

There was a small fish farm in Aloguinsan, with six square blocks of one hundred and fifty metres. Each block contained mainly *bangus,* or milk fish. At the side of every pond there were also lobsters, king prawns, mud crabs, blue swimmer crabs, and other varieties of fish. We were disappointed to hear about Papa not being able to come to Australia, but we understood the reasons given. I found out later that it had been Mama's idea not to let Papa come to Australia, in retaliation or revenge after an argument they'd had. Papa was disappointed, but he is a unique person, very understanding, and he happily let Mama go without him.

John contacted the travel agent in Launceston and asked if we could change the name on Papa's ticket to mine, so I would go home to the Philippines, pick Mama up from Aloguinsan, and then fly back to Australia with her. So a week into the summer school break, John took me to the airport, bound for the Philippines. I felt so excited about going back to my family in Aloguinsan for seven weeks! This was something I really looked forward to after a year away from home. However, after only four days with my family and friends, somehow I had feelings of loneliness; I felt something was missing in my life. I really missed John, as well as the place I now called home. I sent a telegram asking John if we could shorten my holidays. Unfortunately, it was impossible, unless we were willing to cover the cost of the alteration. Some of John's old friends expressed concern that I would not come back from the Philippines. John, thankfully, did not entertain any such thoughts, being absolutely sure that I would be coming back.

Eventually, of course, my Mama and I did arrive back in Savage River, six days before school started for the new year. I spent the days preparing schoolwork—such as lesson plans, projects for sewing, recipes for cooking—and catching up with my very overdue household chores. Mama helped me with the schoolwork and cooked dinner for us, which was much appreciated. Surprisingly, the piles of schoolwork did not worry me at all, as long as I was in Savage River with John and my new friends.

As usual, every weekend we would pack up our things and go somewhere for a few days' break. Mama was not happy with our lifestyle, comparing it to the life of an itinerant, on the move all the time. She pleaded with us to change our way of life; to have a family of our own. She thought we would be surprised at how happy and inspiring life became if we had a family. John was not so sure that having a family was a good idea. He was very concerned about leaving me burdened with a child if he died. "I am worried about having a family at my age," he told Mama.

I began my second year of teaching with some apprehension, terribly overloaded and busy, but overall at ease. I was thoroughly enjoying my life as a teacher and a wife, and having the company of my mother. I was looking forward to another year's challenge. I took notice of all advice given by my superiors and colleagues, especially the Home Economics teachers from the North West Coast of Tasmania. We met three times a year during Teachers' Moderations. The teachers involved in moderation did their best to make me feel at ease and gave as much assistance as they possibly could. I am very grateful to all of them; they were terrific, amazing people and exceptionally helpful. I would especially like to mention the President of the Association, Mrs Pat Coy, as well as Mrs Andrea Cox, the Association Secretary.

Looking back, I think I must have been the silliest individual that God ever created. Why on earth did I accept all those jobs? They were definitely time-consuming, and amazingly I still had energy to pack our things on Fridays to go places for our weekend breaks.

The three of us had a great time in Savage River. Mama enjoyed being in John's company; they really clicked, and it was a shame that Papa was not with us. I was very spoiled; for three months I had the undivided attention and undivided love from my mother. When I was at school and John was at work, my friend Gale would keep Mama company. Mama liked Gale very much and vice versa. They went everywhere together: shopping, picnicking, or just wandering around town.

Eventually it was time for Mama to pack her things and go back to the Philippines, "where I belong", as she would say. Although it was summertime, for Mama it was freezing cold, especially as Savage River had four seasons in a single day, and it was always wet. She could not stand the cold. Also, she really missed Papa. This was the first time they had been separated in the whole time they had been married. I thought it served her right, really, but I never said anything to her; she would definitely have killed me. I hated to think about the fact that Mama was leaving us the following week. Secretly I was crying every night in bed.

In April, early one morning, John, Mama and I headed off to Launceston, where we stayed overnight before boarding the first flight to Melbourne. Mama's flight to Manila was scheduled early in the afternoon on 3 April. Unfortunately, our flight from Launceston was delayed for an hour for some reason, and so we arrived in Melbourne an hour late. We had lunch in one of the restaurants in the airport and then went to buy a souvenir for Mama to take home from the duty-free shop. Mama found her handbag rather heavy with the souvenir, so we decided to check it in along with her normal luggage. While we were checking Mama's luggage, airport personnel announced that the aircraft bound for Manila was desperately waiting for a passenger by the name of Mrs Maria Pielago! The aircraft was already closing its doors, ready for take-off. The airport personnel took Mama swiftly to the counter and then down to where the Philippine airliner was already taxiing. We were informed that Mama's luggage was still at the airport counter and would not be flying with Mama but on the next available flight, the following day. The gentleman at the counter was very apologetic and guided us to where we could see the aircraft taxiing onto the runway.

I was extremely upset that I had not had a chance to say goodbye to my Mama, or even give her a hug. Looking back, everything that happened was God's will. He protected both Mama and me from having a heart attack. Heaven knows what would have happened if Mama had departed in the usual relaxed way.

CHAPTER 6

The school's annual ball had been set for Tuesday, 17 August. Mr Bellchamber, one of the senior masters, was in charge of the event. He had to make sure the students were well rehearsed in all steps of the twenty-five ball dances. Every recess, lunch, and physical education session was spent practicing those dances. Everyone from the year sevens to year tens had to be involved in the dancing; no excuses were accepted. Of course, all the staff were also involved. A few times, yours truly was asked to help supervise the children during their dance rehearsals. It was incredible to watch the children dancing gracefully. The waltzes . . . I could have watched the all day, every day. It was truly wonderful, and I really looked forward to seeing the students wearing gowns and tuxedos, with the gentlemen bowing to the ladies and the ladies curtseying.

The students, with the help of the staff, decided to name the event Knots and Crosses. As a member of the teaching staff, I was required to supervise. I had not attended any formal affairs recently, not since my junior and senior proms at university. Therefore, I did not have any formal attire for this special event. Luckily, when I had left the Philippines, Alma had packed my haltered, beautifully made, apricot-coloured dress, saying, "You might need this someday. Just store it in your wardrobe for when you need it." She was right. That night I wore what the locals would call an after-five dress, matched with gold-coloured, two-and-a-half-inch-high sandals, a white pearl necklace, and matching earrings. John was very admiring of my outfit as he dropped me off at the event. Unfortunately, he was just about to start his afternoon shift and was not able to be my escort.

Mr Julius Kearon, the school's Principal, officially opened the night and welcomed the guests. Then he passed the microphone to the Master of Ceremonies, Mr Bellchamber. The evening began with a progressive dance, followed by a Pride of Erin; and it ended with a waltz. The girls—well, ladies—looked just gorgeous, and the boys, or young gentlemen, were so handsome.

They all danced so gracefully while their parents watched them, full of pride. Who would not be? During the intermission, the Master of Ceremonies announced that the students and staff would be searching for the recipient of the title Matron of the Ball. I had a feeling that the students were up to something, so instead of sitting in front where I had been seated before, I moved to sit in the back row with my friend Mrs Berent, who was one of the parents attending the event. We were chatting together when my name was called to go up to the stage. It seems I had been unanimously voted Matron of the Ball 1982. Five Grade 9 and 10 students came to escort me to the stage. The crowd's reaction was overwhelming. I was extremely embarrassed and became very shy at facing the Master of Ceremonies, the students, and their parents. I have no idea how I got to the stage. I should have been full of pride and joy, but all I could feel was nervousness and shyness; I was wishing I wasn't in that ballroom. But it was too late for that, Teresita.

The Master of Ceremonies presented me with flowers and a cookery book, which had been donated by the school staff. The children were ecstatic and proud that Mrs Lipsius had been selected as Matron of the Ball. John had been informed by his colleagues, so when he arrived home at midnight, he surprised me by congratulating me straight away. The school's social was a success; it was the talk of the town for weeks.

There was one more event to come: during the last term of the school calendar, the School Fun Day Open Days were scheduled for the second week in November. Plans for the Open Days had been submitted at the end of the first term, so I had no choice. However, it seemed that everything was falling into place. The students were as excited as their Home Arts teacher was. It was actually a huge, daunting challenge, not only to the students, but also for me. All activities were in full swing. Students were making preserves, such as jams, chutneys, tomato sauces, pickles, and marmalades. Cakes and biscuits were to be made a day before the event. They were to be displayed for two days, and people could purchase any of the displayed items, collecting them on the last day of the event. The proceeds of the sales were to be given to the makers. It was a good incentive for the children, inspiring them to make things of good quality in order to attract the attention of customers, most likely the parents. The sewing classes were also busy doing their bit. The younger grades were making embroidered items such as cushion covers, stuffed animals, crocheted table runners and doilies, fancy pincushions, pillowcases, aprons, handkerchiefs, macramé and appliqué, while the older students made dresses and outfits for the fashion show.

The students weren't limited; they were allowed to make as many items as they could. The more items the better for display purposes. It was also part of the student' final practical exam. It was actually good timing for their end-of-year marking. They were to be judged by a panel of five members, including the mine manager's wife and other personnel of the Savage River Mine. I had had to ask John for help to solicite prizes, as I knew no one else to approach. The items the students created as part of their practical exam were only to be displayed and weren't for sale.

One night after dinner, John asked, "How's everything at school?"

Before I could answer him, an idea occurred in my little brain: *Grass skirt*. And that very night, the Hawaiian Dance was created. I produced an Hawaiian dance tape and choreographed some Hawaiian dance steps, but who could I get to be the dancers?

The next day, a meeting was called at lunchtime for all Home Art students involved in the Open Days. A rough programme that I'd made the night before was read to them. Anyone interested in dancing the Hawaiian dance was to write her name on the piece of paper provided. The same went for the calisthenics (exercises), but only boys were needed for those. Amazingly, fifteen boys signed up for calisthenics and twelve girls for dancing. A notice of the students' school activities was sent to all parents; it also asked if they could help in any way to make the events successful. For some reason, the draft of the programme was shown to one of the senior masters, the coordinator of the Fun Day. He took it on board and presented it to the Principal, who asked if the school could watch a preview. The preview was arranged, and as the Principal was very impressed, the draft programme became an official one:

PROGRAMME
1. **Welcoming by the Principal**
2. **Speech by Parents and Friends President**
3. **Introduction from the Master of Ceremonies**
4. **Singing Competition**
5. **Fashion Parade, Grade Nine**
6. **Calisthenics**
7. **Fashion Parade, Grade Ten**
8. **Hawaiian Dance, Ending with a thank you speech by Mrs Lipsius**

Only the fashion shows were to be judged; the rest were for entertainment only.

The preparations weren't easy, but they went without a hitch. Fortunately the parents were very supportive and helpful right from the beginning. They helped the children sew their own costumes, especially the grass skirts, which weren't easy. I was very grateful, as without their solid support the event would never have been successful.

The invitation letters, plus others asking for donations of prizes, were sent in plenty of time. None of the invited people refused, and donations poured in. There were more prizes than we needed, so we decided to give prizes for first, second, and third. The school staff helped build the platform for the catwalk, and the basketball court was transformed into a beautiful venue, thanks to both students and staff. The students' works were displayed in the Home Arts room, ready for the public scrutiny, viewing, and purchasing.

The rehearsals for my Hawaiian Dance and Calisthenics were in full swing. Hoops were made for the boys, grass skirts for the girls; everything was being readied for the big event. The final two rehearsals were held at our home, for we couldn't use the school hall any more. Participants were very excited, and it was a struggle to make sure everyone paid attention to all the steps.

The Primary Principal asked if it were possible for all the primary classes to come on Wednesday (the day before the official opening) and view the displays before the public did. I responded with a very big yes—surprised that the students' display was considered worthwhile for the primary children and teachers to see. I began to get very excited and could not wait for the day of the Fun Fair to come.

Savage River District School comprised two sets of school levels: Infant-Primary and High School. Although they were under the same roof, the primary grades were located at the back side of the building, far from the high school, and they had their own courtyard.

The anticipated big day came. John dropped me, with a load of things for the events at the school, on his way to work. I felt helpless; all I could do was to check last-minute preparations. It was very nerve-racking to see the people queuing up outside the gates, waiting for the doors to open. The public were given an hour to wander around the building with a student tour guide. We were never short of volunteers for this job; the students were so proud to do whatever job was available to do. The guides took the visitors to view the displays in the Home Arts room. They could purchase items if they wished to. The proceeds of the sales, after the original costs had been covered, were to be divided amongst the producers, which was a great incentive for the students. The parents, grandparents, carers, and visitors were all very complimentary. They thought the students' work was excellent, and they flattered the Home Arts teacher by saying things like, "Your students are so clever. It is a great credit to you."

The PA sounded for the audience to move into the school hall/basketball court, as the programme was to commence in a few minutes. The announcement echoed all around. The transformed hall was overflowing with people, more than we had expected. The Principal had to order more chairs to accommodate the audience. The judges table faced the platform/catwalk where the fashion parade would take place. The four judges were excited, and the models couldn't wait to do their jobs.

Everything went very smoothly. The Parents and Friends President thanked me, the Home Arts teacher, for making the children proud of what they'd made. They were proud to show off their outfits by modelling them on the catwalk and show off their skills to the public, and the judges in particular. It was the most overwhelming speech I'd heard since I began my journey into the unknown. The event was a big success, the talk of the town for months. As you can imagine, I was dreadfully tired but very satisfied with the outcome. The Principal and the senior masters all personally congratulated me on a job well done.

The following week, the staff were informed that all student reports must be handed in by the second week of November. Well, though I'd not fully recovered from my exhaustion, it was not too difficult for me this time, having had experience the previous year. I had plenty of things to write comments about.

At the end of November I was informed that my appointment would cease at the end of the school year in 1982. A letter from the Department of Education stated that there were plenty of new four-year-trained graduates (teachers), who would be given priority to fill any available positions. Although I had trained for four years in the Philippines, my qualification was only considered as a two-year-training in Tasmania. The thought of not coming back to school and not being with the children the following year was very hard for me to take. John said, "It is understandable, Terrie. You've learned to love and enjoy your job as a teacher, especially the company of the children. Of course you will miss them. I suppose we will have to concentrate on other very important matters in our lives, as Mama urged us to."

The Principal cheered me up somewhat by saying, "Look, we could still be seeing you next year as a relief teacher. The school needs relief most days, if you would be available."

The following year, 1983, John and I seriously began thinking of starting a family. We hadn't discussed it much before, after John had said he didn't want children because of our age difference. He believed leaving me alone to look after a child or children would be too cruel and the last thing he would want to do to his wife. However, after my mama left to go back to the Philippines, John began talking about it one night after dinner. He said that he'd been thinking about what my mama had said, which had been that having children would change our lifestyle to a better, happier, and healthier one. Anyway, that night we made a very important decision, which we've never regretted; it was the best, most wonderful decision we've made in our lives.

We did not waste any time. We planned, if possible, to have a baby on our wedding anniversary in June—though we knew that might well be wishful thinking! We decided to see a doctor at the Savage River Clinic to make sure we were both healthy enough to have a family. John's second-biggest concern was the baby's health. He was very much aware of the incidence of deformed babies born to prime-age parents, having read and heard of several occurrences. John took it very seriously; however, the doctor gave us the green light, saying, "I cannot see any problem for you two in starting a family. You are both exceptionally healthy."

In February, prior to this decision being made, John had booked an open ticket for a trip around Australia by land and sea. Everything was ready and we were just waiting for the warmer weather. We planned to go sometime in October. As I was only a relief teacher, there were no difficulties about when we went.

In the meantime, another couple with two beautiful children arrived at Savage River. The wife was a Filipina, originally from Mindanao, who spoke the same Visayan dialect as I did. There was also another couple, with a pretty little daughter, who came to Savage River just after I did. They were from the Tagalog region of Manila. Unfortunately, as the wife came from Manila, she spoke Tagalog and couldn't understand a word of my Visayan dialect, so we ended up using the English language to communicate.

The three of us had a great time together, enjoying one another's company. Every weekend we would have a get-together at someone's home, just having fun, cooking our favourite Filipino food, talking, and eating. When

I broke the news to these ladies that John had agreed to have a family, they were both delighted. "It is about time, Terrie!" they chorused. One of them even passed on her own experiences of pregnancy, advising me what to do or not to do.

In September, John and I went to the see the doctor, who did a pregnancy test. When she came back from the laboratory, we could tell she had good news to tell us. I was six weeks pregnant! "You can carry on living a normal life. Just take it easy for the first three months, as they can be a bit delicate sometimes, especially as you are not a spring chicken any more," she smiled. I had known that I was pregnant right from the conception in September, but I hadn't told anyone. I'd only gone to the doctor for confirmation of what I already knew.

She referred us to a gynaecologist in Burnie. She told us that he was a good doctor who would look after us; he wasn't much of a conversationalist, but he cared for his patients. She also told us that our child would be due sometime in June. John and I just looked at one another in disbelief—our baby was due on our wedding anniversary? Unbelievable! Neither of us could utter a word; we were totally speechless.

On our first visit to the gynaecologist, he showed us the scan of the baby's heart beautifully beating at regular intervals. John and I were over the moon, ecstatic to hear our baby's heartbeat. On the second visit, he advised us not to go ahead with our planned trip around the country, as it was considered a bit risky. "It is wise to rest for the first few months and avoid stress," he told us. "Although exercise is vital, don't take it to the extreme," I was told. So John advertised our tickets to his colleagues and luckily managed to sell them.

Food cravings had never been in my vocabulary before. I had heard that women apparently craved some foods during their pregnancies, but I had never believed it. I thought the women had made it up to give their husbands something to do. However, four months into my pregnancy, I woke up at about half past eleven at night and couldn't stop thinking about bananas. I had an incredible urge to eat a banana. I really wanted a banana! The difficulty was that it was now midnight and it was absolutely ridiculous to think of eating bananas in the middle of the night! So I tried to ignore this craving, but I ended up waking John and telling him that I just *had to* have a banana to eat. Seeing as it was midnight in a small country town, there were no shops open, so he rang a friend to see if she had any bananas. Luckily she had two, not good-looking ones, but still edible. As soon as John got back from our friend's place, I grabbed a banana and crammed it into my watering mouth. It must have looked as if I hadn't eaten for a week. That banana was the most delicious banana I had eaten in my life. It was incredible! Why had I wanted to eat that banana at midnight? It made me realize that cravings are part and parcel of the experience of pregnancy. It might not happen to every woman, but it definitely happened to me. Thankfully, that was the only craving I had until my child was born.

All fizzy drinks, chocolate, and coffee were off my menu since my child had been conceived—not because I wanted to, but because I couldn't stand the smell. Just looking at my favourite foods made me feel ill. However, I was not the only person feeling ridiculous at that time. The productivity was high at the Savage River Mine, and there were quite a few women expecting. The wife of an engineer at the mine, Mrs Alexander was the coordinator of the pre-natal classes. She was very active in many of the town's activities. She was the most caring person, and she was also expecting a child. She arranged to have one of the midwives from the North West General Hospital in Burnie come and conduct pre-natal classes. The midwife, Sister Helen, was an amazing person, very involved from the moment we first started the classes right up until each child was born. She was always there to give us advice and make us feel at ease and confident. Sister Helen made sure that each of the mums-to-be was as happy, relaxed, and comfortable as possible during the entire period of her pregnancy.

I found it very amusing when we mums-to-be, with our big, round, protruding bellies making us look like snowmen, were marched down to Pieman Place, the unused single men's quarters, where we held our pre-natal classes. In the hall, we had to lie on our backs on our individual rugs and pillows. Our big bellies sticking up in the air reminded me of puffer fish washed out and dried in the sand after a typhoon. It was so funny I couldn't keep it to myself. I told Mrs Alexander, who told everyone else, and we all had a good laugh. We pregnant women were like a very close-knit family, and we looked after each other, especially as the days of our deliveries approached. Everyone in our class was very nice and looked after me as though I were a little sister. They asked me about my opinions and ideas. It was a remarkable feeling to me, the feeling that I was important and that my ideas and opinions were valued. Two women I in particular I want to thank are Mrs Janette Alexander and the midwife, Sister Helen O'Neal. They made an incredible difference in my life during that period of pregnancy.

Sister O'Neal arranged for the husbands to come along to our pre-natal classes. "It is so important for the husbands to be a part, to get involved, and to be prepared for the big event." she would say. The husbands, including my John, came along at least once a week, depending on their work schedules. At their first session, I could not hold my amusement in. I was always the stirrer in the group; I couldn't help it, it was in my nature. I couldn't stop giggling at the way the men were breathing, as if they were some badly prepared rowers, rowing their boats in a race. They looked very peculiar! Well, you can imagine it for yourselves. The husbands also laughed, as they knew themselves that they looked ridiculous. Sister O'Neal was very patient and understanding about the embarrassment of the men, and she calmed everyone down enough to go back to the breathing exercises.

CHAPTER 7

When I was eight months pregnant, we moved into a three-bedroom house up on the North West Coast; this was partly because my gynaecologist had advised us that we should stay close to the Burnie Hospital as the date of the birth got closer. John would have done so even if the gynaecologist hadn't recommended it, for a number of reasons. He didn't believe in, and feels quite strongly against, home birth, as it can be risky for both the mother and child. Also, although the hospital in Savage River had permanent doctors, nurses, and midwives, in case of complications it was a long way to the Burnie hospital.

So we moved closer to the Burnie Hospital because, although it was still a month before the big event, John did not want to take any chances. Friends of ours kindly offered us the loan of their flat in Somerset, which is only about ten to fifteen minutes' drive to the hospital. How lucky we were to be offered a place so close.

A week after the due date, the doctor advised me to be induced. The child was so comfortable in my tummy and didn't want to come out into this enchanting world. The medical staff took me to the delivery room. The child was scheduled to be born at three o'clock in the afternoon, after my waters had been broken. However, after a few hours of labour, there was no sign of activity inside my womb, and the medical team became concerned. In other words, the baby was in distress, and both of us were in danger. After John had signed all the relevant documents, they rushed me to the operating theatre. John was asked if he wanted to be in the operating room, but he declined, as he thought he would be a distraction to me, and he would rather stay outside.

There happened to be a nationwide nurse's strike on that day, so only very limited medical personnel were available to attend even very serious cases. This limited staff meant that one of my medical team was a male nurse, and the others were concerned about whether I would be comfortable with having a male nurse assisting me. I did not really care who assisted, as long as my baby was safe.

My gynaecologist told me that only the lower part of my body was to be anaesthetized, so I could actually witness the birth of my child. So I was awake the whole time. Then came the most amazing, incredible words I'd ever heard: "It's a boy. A healthy boy." I felt as if the whole world had been given to me as a prize. The nervous, but proud, dad came in, his face hardly visible through a medical gown which covered him from head to foot. The doctor handed John the precious bundle, wrapped in a warm blanket. John awkwardly lowered the baby, so I could have a glimpse of my child. Our son was born on 27 June, at seven o'clock at night, weighing 6 lb 12 oz. Somehow, I had overcooked my child during that last week, and as a result he came out with badly wrinkled skin. He was kept in the Intensive Care Unit for a few hours and then transferred to the nursery. After a few minutes in recovery, heavily sedated, I was wheeled to my room.

When talking of names for our child, I had decided on Joanna Marie for a girl, after John and the two grandmothers, who both happened to have the same name. For a boy it would be Jonas, pronounced *Yonas*, which is John's real name in Lithuanian, as well as being my grandfather's name. John had been delighted with my suggestions and couldn't agree more.

So, on 20 October 1984, Jonas Andrew Lipsius, nicknamed Johnnie, was baptized in the Church of Apostles in Launceston. He was four months old. A few of our friends and the boy's godparents were present. His two godmothers and three godfathers were reminded by the priest of the duties of godparents to support, protect, and help Johnnie on his journey through life. The reception was held at the same venue as our wedding had been, the Olde Tudor Inn in Launceston.

Five months after Johnnie was born, my thumb and index finger became incredibly sore, making things like lifting a cup or making coffee a struggle. Everyday chores, like getting a bucket of water for Johnnie's bathtub, were an agony; the pain of my thumb was excruciating. I went to see the local GP. She told me it looked like tendonitis. The GP bandaged my thumb and forefinger together and gave me some medication. I was told to wait for a week or two to see if there was any improvement, but if there wasn't any I might have to be referred to a specialist. After two weeks the pain was still unbearable, so the GP arranged for me to see a specialist. Straightaway I was admitted to the Saint Lukes Private Hospital in Launceston to have surgery on my left wrist. The surgery was successful, and after a few hours in recovery, they transferred me to my room.

I stayed in the hospital for two days and three nights. The first night Johnnie was not allowed to be with me, and it caused a huge problem. He became very upset and cried for hours. Although the nurse took him to the furthest room, I could still hear my son's pitiful cry. John pleaded with the nurse to allow Johnnie to stay in my room, but she refused, reasoning that he might be a problem for me. "Mum needs some rest," she told us. At half past twelve, Johnnie was still crying. The nurse at last brought the boy to my room, worried by the fact that he was so upset and not settling down.

I asked the nurse to put my son into my right arm and let him sleep with me, reassuring her that he would stop crying. As soon as Johnnie was in my arm, he immediately stopped crying. He quickly put his arms around my neck, his face very wet with tears, and went to sleep.

The following morning after his bath, the nurses asked if they could borrow Johnnie; another patient in the surgery ward, who had just had a major operation, would like to see the "gorgeous boy". I agreed, forgetting to ask what time they would be returning him. After about an hour I began getting worried, thinking that my son could have been kidnapped. I alerted John and asked him to look for our son. John was just a few steps out the door when he saw a happy group of medical staff talking to Johnnie on the way back to our room. The medical staff assigned to that area called in to our room every time they were on duty just to give Johnnie a cuddle. He was very popular.

Our next-door neighbour, Wendy, often visited to offer her help or just to chat. She'd make coffee for both of us or look after Johnnie while I had a shower. When Johnnie was nearly six months old, he changed from a happy, satisfied baby to a constantly crying one, and I could not figure out why. Wendy, noticing the change, took him from my arms and tried settling him down by giving him a few drops of honey. The boy licked it with pleasure. "Is it time for the baby to have his feed?" she asked.

I told her, "I only fed him a few minutes ago, but he keeps crying."

Wendy said, "I'm sorry, but I think you might be starving your child. I think you might have run out of milk." I began panicking, but Wendy calmed me down and gave Johnnie some fresh milk in a bottle, which he emptied in no time.

Wendy's children were also a godsend. The accepted Johnnie, played with him, and looked after him lovingly, treating him like one of their siblings.

Johnnie celebrated his first birthday on 27 June 1985 with a few children of his own age; our dearest neighbours Wendy, Gale, and Sid; his godparents; and a few of our other friends. Early on the morning before his birthday, Johnnie managed to walk three steps, to the total delight of his mum and dad. That afternoon he had his first haircut, another milestone.

The following year, in 1986, when Johnnie was only one and a half years old, John decided to retire. Savage River was wholly owned by the mine, meaning that it was a company town where only employees of the Savage River Mine resided. So we had to leave and find a new place to live. It was not easy to say our goodbyes to our friends. The mining company gave us a farewell party; the company, John's colleagues, and the community presented us with some valuable parting gifts. It was a mix of emotions for us. I had called the place home for five daunting, enchanting, exciting, and happy years of my life, but now we had to move on.

We bought a house in Burnie, and a take-away and general store in Cooee, a suburb of Burnie. Our new house was on a hillside, about a hundred metres above sea level; it was a most unique spot. The first few days in our new home felt unreal, like a fairy tale, particularly at night when the town and port were lit up. We loved the place and are still thankful that we own this little slice of paradise on earth. The city of Burnie, with a population of about twenty thousand, is a vibrant commercial, industrial, and cultural centre, partly due to the fact that the port of Burnie is the busiest deep-water port in Tasmania.

Our new business was situated opposite Burnie High School; it served very like a canteen, in that we dealt mainly with students. We would have about five hundred students coming to the store for breakfast, recess, and lunch. There had been two previous owners. Mr Dickenson had built the shop when the high school was constructed in 1950, and we had bought it from the second proprietor. John hadn't been overly enthusiastic about the prospect at first, but considering our available capital and my experience during my university days in the Philippines—where cafes, take-away, and canteens near a school were a gold mine—we decided to buy. We soon discovered that the business was not as profitable as we had thought. Only a few locals came for groceries like bread, milk, and other essentials. We did try to build the business up, but unfortunately the shop's location was too far out of the way to attract customers. So we basically depended on the students, and this was not profitable enough.

Running the take-away was a full-time job. We opened at seven o'clock in the morning to prepare the food for the day. The routine was unbelievable, especially at recess and lunch, when it would be so busy we could only spend a few seconds on each customer. Recess was exceptionally busy, with students putting in the lunch orders as well as purchasing snack food for their morning tea. We carried hundreds of chocolate bars, confectioneries, chips, all sorts of hot and cold drinks, hot chips (lunch only), hot foods, sandwiches, desserts, and ice creams. There was one particular drink that I hated most; it was called a spider. The name itself made me hate it. It was very difficult and awkward to prepare. You had to be extra careful to add the ice cream into un-fizzed lemonade, or it would somehow become a fountain, cascading like Niagara Falls onto the preparation table, leaving not a drop in the glass. Every cafeteria worker who has to prepare this drink will know what I am talking about. Heavens knows who invented this funny drink, which everyone seemed mad about. Actually, I have to agree that it is a refreshing drink; it's just that it's very difficult to make.

Life at the shop with a little one was not "a piece of cake". No matter what was in store for John and me, our son was always a priority. Time moved quickly, and we celebrated Johnnie's second birthday with a few friends at our new home. After we settled down a bit and got used to the routine, my attention focused on my son's education. An hour every morning was set aside solely for education and another in the afternoon for children's TV programmes. The rest of the day was for rest, play, and some learning. All big bold letters from boxes were cut out and collected. Johnnie thoroughly enjoyed cutting these coloured letters from the boxes. I bought from Toy World an abacus for counting and a blackboard and ABC letters as an alphabet guide. I glued the letters of the alphabet to the blackboard for him to follow. I could easily have bought him some fancy flash cards, but I wanted the boy to enjoy the process at the same time as he learned them by heart. It was fun, simple, and very effective. By the age of three Johnnie could count from one to ten, had memorized all the letters of the alphabet, and was able to write his full name.

Our son grew up in a loving, if rather busy, environment. Johnnie watched, observing his Mummy and Daddy working hard to make ends meet. Running the business plus managing every day's household chores was a hard job. The best thing about this time was that the three of us were together from the time we opened at seven o'clock to when we closed at five in the afternoon. Just having our son with us was very satisfying, making our exhaustion just fade away.

In November 1988 I thought of a special thing for Johnnie to do on Christmas Day. The boy was four and a half years old; what about if he gave flowers to the sick people in the local hospital? I mentioned it at the dinner table and explained to Johnnie the reason for giving flowers to the sick. If he was happy to do it, we would start that very Christmas. His reaction was very positive; in fact, he was delighted at the prospect. On Christmas Eve, I collected flowers, mainly roses, from our garden and our friends', plus from the high school. After dinner I started the painstaking job of removing all the thorns from the rose stems before making the bouquets. I stopped to attend Midnight Mass, and then I continued until all the flowers were done. At nine o'clock on Christmas Day, Johnnie and I were at the hospital (the same one where he had been born) with five laundry baskets full of beautiful bunches of flowers. I asked the medical staff if Johnnie could give flowers to the patients, and they happily agreed. Unfortunately a "red gentleman", Santa Claus, was a few minutes ahead of us. He was loaded with presents to give the patients. He spotted Johnnie and gave him some lollipops. I asked whether we could go first to deliver our flowers, but he refused. I was a bit annoyed, because we had to wait until Santa was gone.

There were strict instructions from the Head Nurse regarding the boy's safety; someone had to accompany him and hand the flowers to the patients. He also had to wear a mask when entering some of the patients' rooms. There were plenty of volunteers to assist him. The nurses, doctors, and other hospital staff on duty were ecstatic to see Johnnie giving flowers to the sick. Both patients and staff thrilled when the boy greeted each person with, "Merry Christmas. I have flowers for you." Patients responded emotionally, giving the boy a hug or a kiss, wishing him a bright future, blessing him, and offering him prayers. They were the most heartfelt responses you could ever hear or see. It has become an annual event for us, which we still continue—but we make sure we are in the hospital half an hour earlier to beat Santa!

When Johnnie was eight years old, a very frail gentleman, who was about to be flown by air ambulance to the Hobart Hospital, insisted on seeing the boy who was giving flowers before he would leave his room. Wearing a medical gown and mask, Johnnie was escorted to the patient. The gentleman thanked Johnnie, blessed him, and wished him all the best in whatever his future held. Johnnie resumed distributing the flowers. At our last stop, a nurse came over to us and explained that, sadly, the gentleman had passed away before his flight had reached Hobart. Johnnie did not utter a word. I don't know whether he didn't comprehend what had happened or whether he was shocked by it.

CHAPTER 8

Another very important family tradition of ours is attending Midnight Mass on Christmas Eve. It is a very important event in the Catholic calendar. After Mass, we would go home and open our presents, which we were very excited about. We never missed a Midnight Mass from the time we moved to Burnie till 2010, when for some reason, a Vigil Mass was celebrated at ten o'clock instead of a Midnight Mass. I had been informed of the change, but somehow it had completely slipped my mind, so we went to church as usual at half past eleven and were most surprised to find it dark and closed. It was unbelievable. I sat on the steps in the car park, very upset, and refused to believe that there was no Midnight Mass.

John participated in church activities, attending Mass on Sundays, Johnnie's first Holy Eucharist and Confirmation, and any school Masses. Johnnie and his father religiously recited evening prayers together before Johnnie went to bed. Even when Johnnie got older and memorized the prayers, they would still say them together.

In 1989, when Johnnie was five years old, we enrolled him in the kindergarten at Burnie Primary School. This official start to his education was a very important milestone in his life, but the first time John took Johnnie to school it was also a very emotional day for me the. Watching my son carrying his tiny Thomas the Tank Engine school bag was enough to trigger tears. My baby wasn't a baby any more—he was beginning to grow up. He began by attending three afternoons a week. As the year progressed, the school increased the attendance to two hours in the morning and two hours in the afternoon. The kindergarten teachers were very pleased that Johnnie was able to recognize the alphabet, could write his name, and could read simple story books, not just picture reading. He was also very likable, well-mannered, and friendly to everyone; he developed close bond with his classmates.

The following year he transferred to Stella Maris Catholic Primary School, where he had been originally enrolled but hadn't been able to attend, as they hadn't had kindergarten at that time. It only accommodated prep to Grade 5. The sixth grade, normally the final primary year, was run at the big school, Marist Regional College.

Johnnie completed Grade 5 in 1995; he was School Captain for the year. It was also the year that the Catholic School Board decided to transfer the Grade 6 classes to Stella Maris. The 1996 Grade 6 class was the first to complete their primary education at Stella Maris. It was quite a historical event for the school, and Johnnie was part of it. Of course, the following year, Johnnie went to Marist Regional College for Grade 7.

The year of 1999 was a disastrous year for me and my family, both emotionally and financially. Every year in December, as a normal practice, we reduced the stock in our shop to practically nothing except for the grocery section used by local customers for essential items. A few weeks before school started, we restocked the shop, ready for the school's opening that year. Six days before the first school term started in February 1999, Burnie High School's Principal came and informed us that the students would not be allowed to come to our shop any more. John and I were dumbfounded and shocked by the news. I asked, "Why?"

The Principal answered, "The school is worried about the safety of the children."

I replied, "Fair enough, but why did you not warn us last year before the school's break-up, so we wouldn't spend thousands of dollars on new stock? Why only tell us now? You come only six days before school starts. We cannot stop the school from doing this, but please be fair to us. We did not do anything wrong, or anything that would jeopardize students' safety in our shop."

He listened, but at the end he said, "It was agreed by the school that as soon as the students' arrive at school in the morning, they won't be allowed to leave again. The school canteen can provide the food for breakfasts as well as recess and lunch."

I felt like screaming to let go the lump in my throat, but no sound and no tears came out. Monday came with a very unusual scene. Teachers patrolling outside the school fence, in front of the shop, duty teachers directing the students to go straight to the school. John and I went to see the school Principal to see if there was anything he could do to keep us going long enough to finish the first term. He agreed that I could go to the school at recess to get student lunch orders in front of the main building, and deliver those orders at lunch time. It was very humiliating as well as awkward and difficult. Imagine carting lunch orders across the road! However, I didn't mind too much as long as we had some income to keep us going until the end of term. During the school holidays, the town council upgraded the road around the high school and in front of our shop, providing a passageway especially for the comfort and safety of the students crossing to and from the shop. Unfortunately, ultimately it did not help us.

Johnnie had just started his year ten at Marist Regional College. There was still a long way to go in his education, and John and I were very concerned about our son's future. On my way to the school to get the students' lunch orders, tears were running down my cheeks. John's eyes were misty as well as he watched me walking toward the school gate. It had become an everyday occurrence. Early in April the Principal came and informed us that the students could now collect their orders and purchase food at lunch time, but emphasized that it was *only* at lunchtime. I still had to get the orders at the school. John and I were a bit relieved; every little bit helped.

However, we were so desperate, we couldn't think of any other solution than to close the shop at the end of the term. We were losing money every day. We still had to pay rent, and the electricity bill was still the same as before, as we were still using the same fridges, freezers, vats, and lights. We couldn't even sell the business, as it was so unprofitable.

The students noticed the difference in our stock close to the end of the term. However, we didn't tell anyone about the fate of our business, as we didn't want to get the students involved. As John said, it was between us and the school. We wanted to protect the students; we knew they liked us and enjoyed coming across to a friendly, fair, firm, and happy environment. They were happy to come across for a few minutes, just to stretch their legs and get out from the classroom environment. Even just accompanying their friends, without buying anything, it was enough to have a breath of fresh air and say, hello to Mr and Mrs L (short for Lipsius).

The school Student Council collected signatures from more than three quarters of the school's student population on a petition to get the school to reverse the new rules. They showed the petitions to us and asked us to sign, but we had to refuse. Some parents thought it would be a good test of the Student Council to see if they could reverse the changes. The parents were in favour of letting their children cross the road. "They are not little ones. They are young adults. Besides, there is no traffic in Fiddler Street. It is a no-through road; the only people who use it are teachers." A reporter from the local newspaper contacted us and asked if they could interview us. We refused for the same reason that we wouldn't sign the petition: "It is between us and the school. If you want to write about it, go and interview the school's Principal," John told them.

It was a struggle, but we tried to stay calm and healthy, not to become overly stressed, for the sake of our son. We tried to shelter Johnnie from the crisis as much as we could. He was aware of what was going on, but we made him promise to concentrate on his studies. "Leave the problem to us. Hopefully everything will be all right in the end," we told him. We assured him that his education was a priority no matter what; it would never be jeopardized. Johnnie trusted us and respected our wishes.

The students' petition was unsuccessful, and we closed the shop on the last day of the first term of 1999. It was like the end of our world. The following day we had an auction of all the small items like crockery, cutlery, some of the leftover small goods, drinks, groceries, and confectionery. Luckily, all of it sold. John contacted the scrap-metal people and asked if they could come and remove all the fridges, freezers, mats, anything metal in the shop. They could have it all for nothing; we just wanted to get rid of it. They agreed to come and collect it all by Friday.

That week it was as if someone had died. I couldn't stop crying; I was very worried about our future. Both John and I tried to behave normally when Johnnie was around. I suppose he was aware of what was going on, but he acted as if nothing special was happening, helping us clean and clear the shop as much as he could. I had a mental block at this time. Prayer had always been my shelter and consolation at times like this, but now I found it was impossible to concentrate. I choked and could not say a word; tears blinded me all the time; all I wanted to do was cry. On the Thursday of the second week of clearing the shop, I had a dream, where I heard a voice say three times, "I will never shed a tear again about the shop." Early on the Friday morning, while I was in the bathroom, I saw three images of

Christ on the wall. They were my favourite picture of Christ: the Sacred Heart of Jesus. One image was in front of me, another was at the side of the bathtub to my right, and the third was above my eye level, next to the window. They stayed there until we left home to head to the shop, but again, because I was overwhelmed with sorrow and grief, I did not attach any significance to it.

John and I had always eaten our meals at the dining table, with a table setting like that of a four-star restaurant. When Johnnie was big enough to have his meals with us at the table, it was more enjoyable and comfortable to discuss any family matters at the table while we had our meal. I have always loved the feelings of togetherness and closeness we experienced while discussing important things at the dinner table. After each meal, Johnnie would say, "May I be excused, Mum?" or, "May I be excused, Dad? Thank you for the beautiful meal." What a pleasant reward for the cook. Although it was an everyday occurrence at our home, it was still like music to my ears. I loved it.

That Friday night at the dinner table, the same day I had seen the images of Christ, Johnnie enquired about the fate of the shop for the first time. John reassured him, "If we stay strong, everything will be fine. Tomorrow we are going to Hobart for a week's holiday. While we are in Hobart, no one is to mention business. We are just going to enjoy our stay." John had rung the Federal Casino in Hobart and booked for eight days' accommodation. The three of us had a wonderful time. We cruised around the harbour and visited an Australian frigate, where we talked to the crew members on board. We walked on the beach and had food whenever we felt hungry. We enjoyed concerts while having lunch at the courtyard.

When we got back to Burnie, we continued cleaning and clearing the shop premises, but the atmosphere was very different. My heart was as light as cotton; I was even looking forward to handing back the premises to the owner at the end of the week. I didn't shed a single tear after our holiday, ever again, about that business. There were no negative emotions at all when we handed back the keys. John and I felt as if thorns had been pulled from our bodies; it was a feeling of great relief.

Gardening—upgrading my rose garden and looking after my two hundred pots of orchids—was my first project after closing the shop. Regrettably, after only three weeks, the honeymoon with my garden was over. I needed to do something more fulfilling than that.

Wondering how I could start up my stagnant brain again after so many years, I remembered someone mentioning TAFE (Technical and Further Education) Tasmania, but because it was nearly the summer holidays, not many courses were being offered. Only one course was available every summer, a call-centre course. It was mainly about using communication tools, like the computer, and telephone skills, which was not much to my liking. We had owned a computer since Johnnie had been in primary school, but I had never thought of learning how to use it. During my education there had been no computers, and I felt it was a bit late for me to start studying computers at my age. However, it was the only choice available, so I enrolled at TAFE for a four-week course. My teacher assured me that help was always available if I needed it; all I had to do was ask. She was incredible; most of the time she gave up her free time to council and coach me during her break. She encouraged me to keep going when I was depressed and wanted to quit. I had to learn very quickly due to the limited time. After four weeks of hard, tearful, nerve-racking work, I graduated.

Graduating this course encouraged me to believe that I could do other studies. In January, I decided to upgrade my teaching qualification and enrolled at the Launceston campus of the University of Tasmania to do a Bachelor of Education in-service course. The University acknowledged both my schooling in the Philippines and my experience in Savage River, giving me 50 per cent credit, but I had to study for the remaining 50 per cent in order to become an accredited four-year trained teacher. Although I had trained for four years in the Philippines, in Tasmania it was only considered equal to a two-year course, as I mentioned earlier.

The first few days and months of my in-service studies were very difficult. Unbelievably, I managed to cope with the pressure of meeting due dates of assignments, reading, writing essays, attending lectures, you name it—it was more than a nightmare! There was no such thing as UniStart then, which is now available at the three Tasmanian campuses. I had never heard of it, in any case. UniStart is a preparatory course for people who are not sure how to study at university, what to expect, and what skills are needed to succeed. It would have made things much easier for me. My biggest problems were writing and structuring essays, summarising and paraphrasing, referencing, Internet searching, and time management. UniStart now teaches all that.

Orientation Day was my first day at the Launceston campus of the University of Tasmania (UTAS). It began at four o'clock in the afternoon and went until ten o'clock in the evening. There were twenty students in the room that afternoon. Nearly all of them were experienced teachers currently working in Tasmanian schools, but like me, they were only two-year trained. They had been told that they should either study for a four-year degree or face retrenchment. There was a surplus of new four-year trained graduates, so all my classmates were practicing teachers. As you can imagine, I was terribly nervous, sitting in the corner of the lecture room, surrounded by all these experienced teachers. I was like a dog with its tail between its legs.

After the introductions, we were asked to think of something that we would like to share with our classmates and then write an essay of sixty to seventy words on that topic in the next fifteen minutes. The essay would then be read to the class, followed by feedback from the critics. Since I had not had any university preparation, nor had I worked as a teacher for nearly two decades, half my brain cells had gone kaput. My perspiration soaked my singlet in spite of the cold wintry night, but I was determined to have a go at this essay. At first I had no idea where to start, but at last my brain opened up and I began to write: *Here I am in the corner of the classroom, instructed by my teacher to write an essay. My pen is ready to write, but my brain does not give a signal of what to write. The scary part is hearing the screeching of pens, fellow students scribbling something on their papers. Have faith in yourself, Teresita.* Time was up; we were asked to exchange essays with those next to us and to read theirs. I was very reluctant to give up my work, as I was sure it was hopeless and made no sense whatsoever. Actually, I literally refused to give it to the person next to me. The lecturer noticed the commotion; he said that if I was not comfortable, not to worry about it now, maybe some other time. However, he then asked if he could look at it. After reading it, he commented, "This is good. Very simple but effective." He asked if I minded if he read it to the class. Wow! It gave me a bit of hope and the courage to go on.

One of the subjects available that semester was School Based Curriculum Development (SBCD). The lecturer was a professor, a doctor of philosophy. My first impression of Dr Hamilton was that she was like Hitler. She was a very firm, hard-to-please individual, as hard as the toughest Australian blackwood, yet once I got to know her she was the most understanding and supportive lecturer I encountered in my life as a student. As you can imagine, my first assignment was not anywhere near my professor's standard, and without mercy she returned it to me to be resubmitted in three weeks' time. On the attached noted she advised me to attend a lecture on how to write an essay. She pointed out that one of my subjects dealt with that topic. "Please contact the staff secretary about it." At first I thought she was being unfair, me being the only non-practicing teacher/ student in her class. I felt she should be a bit more lenient. All I could think in my desperation was that I couldn't do it; I was hopeless; I should not be at university; it was the wrong move—therefore, the only solution was to quit. It sounds as if the *quit* word was my last rite at university, but by the end of the day I had realized that the Professor was doing it the hard way in order to make me fully understand the course right from the beginning: how things are done at the university level.

Using a computer for research was another humungous problem. Although I had attended the call-centre course at TAFE, it was not enough. Not all of those lessons were on computing; most of them were on customer service. Luckily, the Faculty of Education decided to set aside one whole Saturday for a computer study class.

Professor Hamilton was an iron lady with regard to assignments and punctuality about submissions, but she was kind at heart. All she wanted was for me to achieve my goal. She guided me on my rough journey with a firm hand, and at the end of my second year I achieved the most wonderful, unbelievable mark from my professor, a Credit+. That was my turning point, that Credit+; my brain began functioning again. I suppose it didn't mean much in the grand scheme of things, but for me it was a miracle. From then on, most of my marks were a credit, distinction, or high distinction. What an amazing turnaround it was for me! Without Professor Hamilton's guidance and her faith in me, I would never have been able to achieve it.

CHAPTER 9

Before the collapse of our business in 1999, I had signed up to be a candidate for the Grande Fiesta Queen at the Grande Fiesta Ng Filipino 2000, to be held in Latrobe for the North West Coast region of Tasmania. It was one of the biggest events organized by the Filipino community in the North West Coast region, and it was sponsored by the Latrobe Rotary Club. Actually, it was a state-wide event, and we were joined by the Filipino communities of Hobart, and Launceston. As part of this pageant I was interviewed on stage, and participated in the fashion parade, having to strut up the catwalk in National Filipino costumes. I was overwhelmed, happy, and full of pride when I was successful and crowned Grande Fiesta Queen 2000. My family was very proud of my achievement;. Winning a pageant was a truly unforgettable and remarkable event.

In that year I was heavily involved in fundraising, organized mainly by the Rotarians from Latrobe. They worked very hard to help the Filipino Organization and the community in general. I greatly admire them for their involvement; their help was second to none. At the Grande Fiesta 2001, I passed on the crown to a lady from Launceston. I was assisted by the Governor of Tasmania and the Philippine Ambassador to Australia. It was one of the highlights in my social life since I'd arrived in my adopted country. John and Johnnie took it in turns videoing the event; they were very pleased about it.

In November 2002, when Johnnie was a graduating (Grade 12) student of Marist Regional College, something terrible happened. John had a massive heart attack. Johnnie and I were devastated! John had always been healthy, and now, out of the blue, he had collapsed. He hadn't even been aware that he was having a heart attack; he had gone to the clinic for consultation, as he had felt a bit strange that day. The GP obviously suspected that it was a heart attack; he ordered an ambulance and sent John to the hospital. After three days in hospital, John asked his heart specialist if he could go home to attend Johnnie's graduation. His request was granted, and he managed to attend the Graduation Mass at the Star of the Sea Church in Burnie. The School Captain's parents were usually asked by the school committee to carry the lighted candles to the altar during Offertory. Johnnie happened to be one of the School's Co-Captains. It was one of our proudest moments for John and me, together with the girl Captain's parents, to carry the special lighted candles to the altar followed by the two School Captains carrying their individual gifts. It was a wonderful moment, and we forgot all about John's heart attack.

After the Graduation Mass we proceeded to the Burnie Civic Centre (now the Burnie Arts and Function Centre), for the graduation dinner and ball. It is a practice at the graduation ball that the graduate's first dance partner is his mother, or her father; therefore, I was my son's first dance partner. What a wonderful moment that was. I really looked forward to dancing with my son, but I was a bit apprehensive and concerned, as I had never ever seen my son dance, even when he was a bit tipsy. The MC asked the graduates to get their partners for the first dance. My son came awkwardly to our table, took my hand, and we began to dance. The wonderful moment was unfortunately marred a bit by Johnnie stepping on my toe, flattening it so that I could barely walk back to our table. After I had this memorable dance with my son, John and I headed off home. John was still tired and weak.

Early the next morning I drove John back to the hospital. The following day he was flown by air ambulance to Hobart for a possible bypass operation. That afternoon, when Johnnie phoned the Hobart Private Hospital to see if his dad had arrived there, he was told that there had been no John Lipsius admitted. Johnnie was worried, and he phoned me to ask where his dad was. I had no idea, as I was still on the bus on the way to Hobart, a trip which had been booked and paid for by Ambulance Tasmania. One of the ambulance personnel rang the accommodation in Hobart before the bus left Burnie, to make sure it would be okay for me to arrive late. I was very grateful for this, as it was after midnight by the time I arrived at my accommodation.

When I arrived, I told the lady proprietor what my son had been told about his dad. She rang the public hospital for me and discovered that John had arrived there that afternoon. He was currently in the care of the heart specialist. John explained later that all heart specialists were based at the public hospital and he had been advised by the medical staff that he would be better off there. The same doctors looked after patients at both hospitals, but at the public hospital John was only a few steps away from the heart specialist station.

All wives, carers, and relatives had pre—and post-operation classes for about an hour on two consecutive days. These prepared them for what to expect and what they would need to do before and after the operation. John was scheduled to have his bypass operation on the Wednesday afternoon at two o'clock. He was wheeled to the examination room just before this time for some thorough tests. I stayed on his bed in the ward, nervously waiting for the outcome of the operation. I felt that John would recover quickly, as he was a basically healthy man and usually healed well. After only an hour or so, John was brought back to his room. I thought I must be hallucinating! I had been told that the operation would take quite a while, much longer than only one hour. The heart specialist explained that the operation had been cancelled; John did not need it, as his heart had made its own bypass! It was known to happen but only very rarely. John must be blessed for it to happen to him. I was dumbstruck and could not believe what I had heard. In my heart I thanked my Lord for everything He had done for John. For me it was truly a miracle!

John was kept one more day for observation and then released from hospital. When we got back to Burnie, John retired to bed and I rushed to attend Marist Regional College's Speech Night at the Civic Centre. It was an important night for Johnnie; as a College Captain he had to deliver his final speech after receiving his academic and sporting awards and then hand over to the newly elected School Captain for the following year.

The following year, 2004, was my final year at university, and I did my teaching practical (practicum) in the same year. It might seem strange, but I chose to go to Burnie High School. The previous Principal had resigned a few months after we had closed the business, apparently due to some serious health issues in his family. My main reason for choosing Burnie High was because Johnnie attended Marist Regional College, and I didn't want to mar his reputation in the case that my practicum wasn't successful.

However, my practicum at Burnie High went very well, under the guidance of the Home Economics Coordinator, Miss Welsh, whom I found very similar to my "Hitler" professor at UTAS. When Miss Welsh was doing a job, she came across as a very strict, unfriendly individual, but when we were off campus she was as sweet as honey. At first I misunderstood her unfriendliness, but then I realized that she was like that so I could achieve my goals, and she helped make that happen. I passed my Teaching Practical with flying colours. In fact, I did so well that toward the end of my time, Miss Welsh asked the Vice-Principal if I could take over her classes for three months while she was on her long service leave. After some hesitation, I accepted the offer and taught Home Economics to several classes, from Grades 7 to 10.

It was my final year at university, so you can imagine how busy I was. However, miraculously, I managed it without too many problems, and at the end of that year I was greatly honoured to accept for the second time my Diploma of Education, this time from the University of Tasmania. The ceremony was held at the Albert Hall in Launceston. This time my own family, my husband, John, and son, Johnnie, proudly attended my graduation. John still had one university student left, as by this time Johnnie was a second-year law student. John and Johnnie were delighted and happy standing in the street watching and taking photos of the parade of graduates; all the faculties marched to The Albert Hall, a tradition of the Launceston campus. Then they met me in front of the Hall. A photo of the Crown Princess Mary was on the front cover of our souvenir graduation programme. This was because Princess Mary had been born and raised in Hobart, Tasmania, becoming the Crown Princess when she married the Danish Prince Frederik in 2004. Princess Mary's alma mater was the University of Tasmania.

The following year, in 2005, I took over the position of one of Marist Regional College's Home Economics teachers for terms two and three. She was taking compassionate leave for the rest of the year. Marist Regional College is the only Catholic College in Burnie, and it's one of the elite schools of the North West Coast. It caters from Grades 7 to 12, with eleventh—and twelfth-year students known as Senior College students. Before I took over this job, an ex-Home Economics teacher, Mrs Joyce, had been filling in for a few weeks until the school could find a more permanent replacement. The Principal asked me to observe the Home Economics classes for three days on full pay. Mrs Joyce introduced me to the job; she advised me on what to do and what to expect on Wednesday's Grade 9 cooking day. She told me that the students knew what groups they were in and what duties they had to do, like emptying the rubbish bins and replacing the bins' plastic bags before leaving their bays. Each bay had four students working individually. Mrs Joyce also took me to the second kitchen and introduced me to the kitchen aide. "She is here to help you. Do not hesitate to ask for her help, especially at the beginning of your time here at the College. She knows where to find everything," Mrs Joyce told me.

I was nervous and full of enthusiasm on my first day at the College, on the Wednesday. I didn't know any of the school staff except the Principal, the Principal's personal secretary, and the Financial Manager, but I was determined to have a go, confident that the kitchen aide would be there to help me. The students seemed all right, until the end of the final period of the day, when we were a bit short on time. Some students were still cleaning and drying their cooking utensils when the bell went. Two minutes later, I let them go, as I did not want them to be late for their class-teacher period. As well, I had to go to my own Grade 7 class at McCauley Wing.

When I returned to the kitchen later, the aide looked very, very cross and was quite unfriendly toward me. She accused me of not doing my job and growled that I had not made the students finish their cleaning up and so on and so forth. I agreed that there were two bins not emptied, and the kitchen floor was not as clean as it should be, but it was not really bad. I tried to reason that it had been my first day, and I was not familiar with the routine; I had not known the students' names, and I was sure it would be different next time. "It's not good enough. It's not good enough," she said, walking from one end of the room to the other. "The floor is filthy—not swept properly. You just disappeared! Where were you? You were told by Mrs Joyce to tell the students to empty their bins, were you not?" She spoke as if I were the lowest servant.

I was on my knees, tears flowing, while I swept the floor and emptied the bins. Meanwhile, she danced around the kitchen like a Commander General giving orders. I felt like saying, "Aren't you paid to do this job, as a cleaner or teacher's aide, or whatever?" But because it was my first day, I kept it to myself.

I contemplated resigning my new job, but what reason could I give my family? I was sure that if John found out that I had resigned my job because of this wicked woman, he would march into that kitchen and confront her. She would disappear during the cooking time, being in the other kitchen or anywhere other than in the class where she was supposed to assist me with the children. As the term progressed, I noticed that when the higher grades were doing their practical (cooking) classes, she would be there helping the students. However, when it came to the lower grades, particularly the Grade 7s, most of the time she would pretend she was busy doing something else rather than helping me.

One day, my twenty-six Grade 7s were cooking rice and two-minute noodles. You can imagine the mess! Fortunately, we were not too bad when it came to time management, but no matter how much effort we put into sweeping the floors and wiping the benches, there were still a few damn grains of rice and noodles left behind. It was the Home Economic Department's rule that the teacher must check each of the drawers to make sure the cooking utensils were cleaned and accounted for before the students left their bays. This particular day, five minutes before the bell, I asked the teacher's aide if she could help me. She refused, saying that she was busy washing things in the sink. This was a blatant lie, as there was nothing in the teacher's sink except a single teaspoon, which I had put there only a few minutes before asking for her assistance. She really wanted me to fail, because my failure was her success; she would then have something to tell and report. She was the most conniving, nasty, and rude individual I have ever encountered in my life.

I just hoped she would change her attitude toward me, even if she didn't help me—as long as she treated me with some respect. When I was a child, the first thing my parents had taught me was respect. I now respect everyone, regardless, even to the smallest crawling animals on earth. (Oops—except for bull ants! I have no respect at all for Tasmanian bull ants. I have been bitten twice by them, once on my hand and once on my bottom. It was not funny; it stung so much that I had to soak my behind in vinegar and it still swelled up like a balloon. I could only sit sideways for days.)

One day, in the staff room, I was about to eat my lunch when my attention was caught by one of the other cooking staff, who wanted to question me about the state of her kitchen. She said that after my Grade 7 class there had been a few wet saucepans returned to the cupboard and rice and noodles on the floor, plus a few other issues. "When was this?" I asked.

She answered, "It doesn't matter when. The fact is that the kitchen was not properly swept, and two wet saucepans were returned to the cupboards." I explained that she must be talking about what had happened a month ago; we hadn't had cooking in the new kitchen since. It sounded like a reprimand from a boss, and as some other teachers overheard it, I found it very embarrassing, indeed.

However, the Home Economics Coordinator did not give me a hard time at all. In fact, she was always there for me and reassured me I was doing a fine job. She was my direct boss, and as a department head she had the right to reprimand me if I did do something wrong. She said, "Those people have been very unfriendly to me ever since I arrived at the College as the Coordinator of the Department." She continued, "They have bullied me and treated me like dirt—and now they're doing it to you. I don't want them to bully you like they have bullied me. They have to be stopped." A few other staff members advised me to take the matter to the Principal, but it is not in my nature to take complaints to a superior, unless it is so out of hand it is absolutely necessary.

After several months had passed, I received a phone call at seven o'clock one morning. At the other end of the line, the teacher's aide was sobbing violently. She could hardly speak, she was so upset, because her boss (the Home Economics Coordinator) was very angry at her and would not listen when she tried to explain. The boss hadn't given her a chance to talk. When she had attempted to interrupt, the Coordinator had yelled louder, almost screaming at her. The Aide said to me, "What can I do, Terrie? Should I resign?"

My heart melted, and I was sorry for her. I should have said, "Bravo! Now you know what it is like. It serves you right!" Instead, I calmed her down and promised to talk to the Coordinator. I told the aide not to worry about coming early but to come at her usual time just before the first period of the day. I would prepare everything, all the ingredients and utensils needed for my Grade 8s' practical lesson for the first two periods. First thing, I would see the Coordinator and persuade her to give the aide a chance to explain her side of things. I did do this, and everyone "lived happily ever after". I thought the aide might have learned her lesson, but she has never changed. No matter how hard I have tried, she still strikes every now and then. I did not expect her to like me, but just to recognize and show respect when I greeted her with a good morning or a hello, and not ignore me as if I were invisible. I don't hold grudges, but of course it hurts me and upsets me very much. If I entertained grudges it would eat me up.

Anyway, it's all in the past. I'm now having a ball with the students and the terrific Marist College staff. I feel very spoiled. I can joke with them or ask them something, even if it is not necessary, just to annoy them and talk to them—all, that is, except to my Principal. I have this phobia; I don't know why. I try to avoid talking to her alone if possible.

I always have a mental block, if you like, and end up running out of words. Don't take me wrongly; the Principal is a very nice lady. She runs the College very smoothly and is very friendly and approachable. My phobia probably goes back to my educational experiences when I was young. Some of the school's administrators back in the Philippines were rude and unfriendly; they acted as if they owned the whole universe, and they are likely the ones who put me off to this day.

CHAPTER 10

A year after my graduation, I went back to my beloved hometown of Aloguinsan. Sadly, it was to attend Papa's funeral. Mama had passed away a year before. They were both eighty-seven years old. I knew that if one of them went, the other would soon follow. They were a very close couple; even if they argued during the day, they still shared and slept on one pillow. How incredible! It was very hard for me to take it—no Papa or Mama to greet me when I came home; no more Mama or Papa to kiss me goodbye.

I stayed for another three weeks after the funeral. I spent my time wandering around Aloguinsan and going to the neighbouring places, to Cebu city, and back to Aloguinsan. I saw that the city was becoming more and more modern. High-rise buildings, modern and huge supermarkets, five-star accommodation, modern shopping centres, and restaurants were popping up everywhere. Each time I've been back to visit my family in Aloguinsan, there has been some progress. We used to get our water from wells and springs; now the people are spoiled, and there is no shortage of water. They are all connected to the big source at the Aloguinsan Hydro Plant, a huge reservoir of spring water which supplies the whole town plus neighbouring areas. Kerosene lamp posts are a thing of the past. Now electricity is supplied to the town by the Cebu Electric Company (CEBECO), the oldest and biggest electricity company in the province. Nearly every household now has a telephone, a television, and even transport. It is a bit sad that only a few things are left to remind me of what Aloguinsan used to be, but I am happy and proud of the programme.

Aloguinsan now has its Alodome, which caters for sporting events and hosts various functions. A modern three-storey townhouse has popped up at the foot of the once-neglected Baluarte Park; Baluarte is now a haven for locals and tourists alike. On the corner, which years ago was an empty space where we used to play in puddles, there is now a popular bakery. Tiya Ponting was once the only baker in town. Now people have a choice of four bakeries to choose from in Aloguinsan alone, and all of them offer all sorts of mouth-watering products.

The town has a few hidden beauties which were not known to us years ago. There are beautiful white beaches to relax on and fauna and flora to explore. There is snorkelling, canoeing, caving, and fishing available. You name it, it is available; there are so many activities and places to see that we didn't know about when I was younger. During the month of June, Aloguinsan celebrates its second-biggest annual event, the Kinsan Festival, named after the town's most popular fish. It is when locals and tourists alike flock to the town to celebrate with the most vibrant and colourful festivities.

Aloguinsan also now has three public high schools, which is a real bonus for the battlers who cannot afford to continue their high-school education outside Aloguinsan. For those people who do not want to continue with an academic education, there is a vocational school available. What a transformation and huge difference technology has brought to Aloguinsan.

Four years after my graduation, at the very same University of Tasmania, my son proudly received his Bachelor of Arts and Bachelor of Law at the University's Hall at the Hobart campus. When Jonas's name was called out during the ceremony, I got goose bumps! I felt like screaming and telling all the people in the hall, "He is my son!" I was so happy and proud that my son was now a lawyer. He still had another six months to do, a legal practicum called "articles"; however, he now had his degree, which was the main thing. He can carry that with him wherever he goes. Jonas's achievement was the highlight of all highlights in our lives.

After his graduation, Jonas was blessed to land a job at the Supreme Court as an Associate to a Judge based in Hobart, plus a secondary job as an Assistant and Advisor to a state senator. Jonas is doing really well even at this early stage in his career; he works very hard. John and I are the proudest parents in the world. Who would not be? All our hardships and perseverance have, at the end, paid off.

I feel very emotional when I think that not long ago—it feels like only yesterday—Johnnie kissed and hugged me goodbye on his way to his first day at kindergarten with his Thomas the Tank Engine school bag on his back. Jonas's feathers are now complete. He has got his wings, and he can leave the nest and fly into the big, wide world. He is ready to fend for himself.

As I look back over my awe-inspiring journey, I am so thankful for all the blessings I have received over the years. Now I look forward with hope to another phase of my journey in life.

Hasta la vista,

Teresita Lipsius